D1590016

*Selected Poems*

# James K. Baxter

*Selected Poems*

# James K. Baxter

Selected and edited by
J. E. Weir

Auckland
Oxford University Press
Melbourne     Oxford

Oxford University Press, Walton Street, Oxford OX2 6DP
Oxford   New York   Toronto
Delhi   Bombay   Calcutta   Madras   Karachi
Kuala Lumpur   Singapore   Hong Kong   Tokyo
Nairobi   Dar es Salaam   Cape Town
Melbourne   Auckland   Madrid
and associated companies in
Berlin   Ibadan

Oxford is a trade mark of Oxford University Press

ISBN   0 19 558094 X

Cover designed by Nikolas Andrew
Typeset in Baskerville by Whitcoulls Ltd., Christchurch
Printed in Hong Kong
Published by Oxford University Press
1A Matai Road, Greenlane, PO Box 11-149, Auckland, New Zealand

# Contents

# Introduction

When he was eleven years old James Keir Baxter wrote the following inscription with a rooster quill on the first page of a new notebook:

*Book 1*
*Original Poetry*
*J. K. Baxter*
Born 29th June 1926
Will die when he and Nature sees fit.

For the rest of his life Baxter remained faithful to his vocation as poet, but he became too an increasingly active participant in the political and social events of New Zealand. This twin allegiance gave birth to a body of poetry which puts the events of his life and times into perspective.

His father, Archibald Baxter, was a self-educated Otago farmer of Scottish descent who, despite persecution and suffering, adhered to his pacifist convictions during the First World War. He loved poetry and his son has recorded that he 'recited Burns and Shelley and Byron and Blake and Tom Hood and Henry Lawson when the mood took him . . .'.*

James Baxter's mother had gained a B.A. degree at Sydney University, and had taken the Tripos in Modern Languages at Newnham College, Cambridge. She was a daughter of Professor J. Macmillan Brown, teacher of English and Classics at the University of Canterbury where he became 'a legend for his energy, his prejudices, his utopian writings and works on Pacific ethnology, and his part in shaping the University of New Zealand'.**

With this background it is not surprising, though scarcely inevitable, that the young Baxter should have become a poet. He began to write verse at the age of seven while attending school at Brighton, near Dunedin.

His childhood, during which he appears to have enjoyed some kind of primitive natural mysticism, was a happy one, but he endured a painful adolescence. In 1938, returning with his parents from a stay of almost two years in England and Europe, he found himself ill-at-ease in New Zealand, where his father's pacifism was made to seem disloyalty as the world moved towards war. The experience served to sharpen his intuitive sense of the

* 'Notes on the Education of a New Zealand Poet'; *The Man on the Horse*, p.122
** *Penguin Book of New Zealand Verse* (ed. Allen Curnow, 1960), p.313

gulf which lay between man's ideal of peace and the rigours of living in a hostile world. Some of the best of his early writing in *Beyond the Palisade* (1944), *Blow, Wind of Fruitfulness* (1948), and *The Fallen House* (1953) is a lament for lost tranquillity as he contemplates the guilt and pain of adult existence.

At the beginning of 1944 Baxter enrolled as a student at the University of Otago. In his 'Essay on the Higher Learning' he described his progress during that year and those immediately following:

My mother was a graduate of Newnham College, Cambridge. She studied Old French for her M.A., and enjoyed punting on the Cam. I think she hoped that some day I would climb the ladder of academic distinction, and go there too, go and get some manners, and come back to be a Senior Lecturer. I almost felt I ought to. What else was there to do? I remember also the clear warning she gave me before I arrived at the Registrar's office – 'James, you may meet some girls at University who want you to sleep with them. I'm not saying you will, but you may. Keep away from them. That kind of thing is wrong and it only leads to trouble.' There was a strong, loving wish to be of help behind her words, and I appreciate it better now than I did then. In one sense her prophecy was erroneous. No Otago girl ever tried to rape me. For many long months I searched hard for such a siren, without success. Those iceberg virgins never melted. But my mother had made a correct estimate of her son's character. My ambitions, then as now, were pudendal rather than academic.

But I was seventeen still, and a strange glamour rested on those grey pseudo-Gothic arches. On a lawn that resembled Dante's Limbo one could sit and watch the waters of the Leith Stream sliding endlessly over weirs. And one of those grave, charming, untouchable nymphs might appear and sit down on the green grass and say, 'Hullo' . . . .

Good things came to me from Otago. My incipient alcoholism took wings like a bush fire, leaping fence and river, in the Bowling Green, the Royal Albert, the Captain Cook, the Grand, the City, the Oban, the Shamrock (on Sundays), and the Robert Burns (my best friend had a flat above it). The Furies, those Muses of black-humour poetry, roosted on my doorstep like great scraggy chickens, and never left it again. It is, after all, their proper home. A female medical student taught me another kind of knowledge in her Castle Street lodgings . . . God also, whom I had not met till then, revealed Himself to me one day when I had reached the middle of a disused railway tunnel, in the grip of a brutal hangover. But was any of this a necessary part of the Higher Learning? It is hard to say. Aphrodite, Bacchus, and the Holy Spirit were my tutors, but the goddess of good manners and examinations passes withheld her smile from me.

Well, I had a difficult session with my mother. She felt (rightly) that I was in danger of becoming a hobo, and should return to Varsity to work. I thought (privately) that I had to find out who I was or else take a large dose of strychnine, and that I needed more elbow room to get on with living and writing. I won the duel, but went out afterwards and wept under a gum-tree on the river-flat below the house.

A year or two later, after much apparently useless experience in various factories, farms, dens, bedrooms, pubs and hovels, I travelled to Christchurch, ostensibly to begin a second Varsity career, actually to visit a Jungian psychiatrist. Somehow the Higher Learning still eluded me. I lived inside the spiritual bomb-shelters erected by Rimbaud, Dylan Thomas and Hart Crane. The irrigating river of alcohol flowed continually through my veins ... I worked in a TB hospital and as a copyholder on *The Press*; had something suspiciously like the DT's, and edited a literary page on *Canta*. It was particularly convenient to have access to the *Canta* room for an amorous rendezvous or a place to lie down in when one couldn't stand up. In Christchurch I associated with Denis Glover and Allen Curnow and became a member of the Church of England. This was unquestionably a seeding-time, when I became a man of sorts and ploughed under everything I had ever known, as a farmer ploughs in autumn before the hard frosts arrive.

Later on I married and came to Wellington. Ever since I had failed in Otago to master the Higher Learning, a sense of incapability had gnawed like a rat at my diaphragm. To quiet this rodent, I acquired extra-murally a unit in Greek History, Art and Literature, while working in the Wellington abattoir. After a year or so as a postman (I was sacked from that job when the bosses found me asleep dead-drunk with my head on a full satchel of letters in the Karori post-office) I came to Training College. There I associated frequently with Louis Johnson from whom I learnt to write about the kind of things that make most people silent. It was possible at that time to take two Varsity subjects a year.

This period is a trifle foggy. I gave three Macmillan Brown Memorial lectures. I passed Stage II Latin with the help of an admirable tutor (the Latin was a help to me in reading my missal when I became a Catholic) and passed Stage III English, after two failures, with the help of a tutor in Anglo-Saxon. I can remember trying to convince the long-suffering lecturer in Symbolic Logic that 'p implies q' was a sexual symbol; and I remember more vividly sitting an examination in Stage III English Literature after two days spent on a Home boat drinking gin with the engineer. Well, I got my B.A. and have it still.

Along with a genuine admiration for the character-shaping power of our institutions of Higher Learning – some of the toughest psychotics in the country inhabit those walls – I feel that they have had little effect, except a negative one, upon the processes that make me tick as a writer. Writing, in my case, had proceeded entirely from Lower Learning, learning who one is. And this is not learnt in a lecture-room or library, but in the jails and torture rooms of a private destiny, or conceivably planting potatoes, or conceivably kneeling blindly at the Mass. In fact, I believe that the gulf is so great between these two kinds of learning, that I would never take a permanent job teaching at a University, in case the seed-beds of my life should be turned, by accident, into a concrete playground or the foundation for a building devoted to Aesthetic Research.

*The Spike* (1961), pp.61-64.

By 1958, having previously joined Alcoholics Anonymous, he had already established the perspectives against which the remainder of his life was to be played out. In that year he was awarded a Unesco grant which took him to India and Japan where he was greatly moved by the condition of the poor. The effect of this visit was to make him even more critical of the dehumanizing aspects of contemporary culture.

In the same year he became a Roman Catholic. Of his conversion he subsequently wrote:

I confess that my own conversion controlled by the Spirit of Love who kindles where he desires to kindle, was founded on the natural ground of that utter lack of credulity, that abyss of scepticism which makes me call myself a modern man. Because I doubted all substantial good, it became possible for me to believe in the Unknown God who is also the son of man . . .

Letter to the editor, 29 March 1961.

In that year, too, Oxford University Press published a selection of his poetry under the title *In Fires of No Return*, and his stature as a poet was recognized internationally.

Although he had not written consistently well during the 1950s – chiefly because of the difficulties he experienced in reforming his life after coming off the grog in third-stage alcoholism – he was able to write not only prolifically but with considerable power during the decade of the 'sixties. This new-found strength and assurance is apparent in *Pig Island Letters* (1966).

During 1966 and 1967 he held the Robert Burns Fellowship at the University of Otago. When his tenure came to an end he engaged in catechetical work for a further twelve months. These were years of considerable literary activity provoked by a late encounter with the setting of his childhood and the memory of his ancestors.

At the end of 1968 an event occurred which heralded the last phase of his life. In a dream he heard the call 'Go to Jerusalem!' – a small Maori settlement on the Wanganui River – and faithful to that invitation he left Dunedin with only a change of clothes and a Bible in Maori.

Before taking up residence in Jerusalem in 1969 he engaged in social work in Wellington and Auckland among drug-addicts, alcoholics, the homeless and unemployed. He claimed to have come to a realization that he was 'steadily dying in the comfort of [his] home, smoking cigars and watching television . . .', while there existed 'a really gross and obvious need for some of the people who [were] getting pulled to pieces in the towns to have a sanctuary . . .'.*

In an interview he further elaborated his reasons for withdrawing from the mainstream of New Zealand society:

I do not favour chemical solutions for spiritual and psychological problems . . . But I do recognize that the smashed myths have somehow to be replaced or reconstructed.

That is why I have become a Christian guru, a barefooted and bearded eccentric, a bad smell in the noses of many good citizens.

'A Scorpion Circled by Fire', *Sunday Times*, 16 January, 1972. p.7.

During his frequent forays from Jerusalem to the cities and towns of New Zealand Baxter worked and spoke for the reconstruction of the social order – his most insistent theme being, 'One of the great crimes of society is to be poor.' ('Poet, Philosopher and Commune Patriarch', l.c.). The record of his life at Jerusalem is recorded in *Jerusalem Sonnets* (1970), *Jerusalem Daybook* (1971), and *Autumn Testament* (1972).

The news of his death in Auckland on Sunday, 22 October, 1972, at the age of forty-six, generated a widespread grief. He was buried in the tribal-ground of the Ngati Hau at Jerusalem, having bequeathed to his countrymen a blueprint for social reconstruction and a body of poetry and prose which was remarkable for its range and level of achievement.

Baxter's early poetry, while demonstrating an unusual facility with language, is largely founded in that obscure, subjective quarrel with life which is so common a feature of a young poet's verse. During the late 1940s and 1950s his output lessened as he concentrated upon achieving technical excellence. At the same time, much of his poetry remained too derivative – he was seldom able to transcend the literary influences of W. B. Yeats, George Barker and Dylan Thomas (whose book, *Deaths and Entrances*, was carried by Baxter 'in the inside pocket of my working coat – through the iron works, the freezing-works, the pubs – drunk and sober – until those poems were part of the structure of my mind.') ('With Stubble and Overcoat'; *N.Z. Listener*, 1364, 26 November, 1965. p.25).

By the early sixties however, Baxter had assimilated techniques from Louis MacNeice, Lawrence Durrell and, at times, Robert Lowell without falsifying his own vision. In terms of literary style he gradually moved away from the gravely rhetorical to the easy vernacular – thus allowing his extraordinary poetic talent to give expression to a range of poems which refuse to restrict themselves

* 'Poet, Philosopher and Commune Patriarch', Auckland *Sun*, 23 October, 1972.

xiii

to the reader of academic, introspective or lyric verse. In the course of his search for personal integrity Baxter had learned to abandon rhetoric in favour of poetic honesty. As a result, in the last ten years of his life he acquired his own voice, and from his various quarrels with God, self, society and death emerged a body of work which reveals him to be not merely the most complete poet to have lived in New Zealand, but also one of the great English-language poets of this century.

*     *     *

During his life James K. Baxter wrote more than 2,600 poems of which 774 were included in his *Collected Poems*. This selection of 248 poems aims at presenting the best of his poetry while giving some idea of its range.

I undertook the task with the permission and warm encouragement of Jacquie Baxter and was assisted in it by Gerard Crotty. My thanks are due to both of them.

J. E. Weir

## The Mountains

In this scarred country, this cold threshold land,
The mountains crouch like tigers. By the sea
Folk talk of them hid vaguely out of sight.
But here they stand in massed solidity
To seize upon the day and night horizon.

Men shut within a whelming bowl of hills
Grow strange, say little when they leave their high
Yet buried homesteads. Return there silently
When thunder of night-rivers fills the sky
And giant wings brood over loftily and near.

The mountains crouch like tigers. Or they wait
As women wait. The mountains have no age.
But O the heart leaps to behold them loom!
A sense as of vast fate rings in the blood. No refuge,
No refuge is there from the flame that reaches

Among familiar things and makes them seem
Trivial, vain. O spirit walks on the peaks!
Eye glances across a gorge to further crags.
There is no desire. But the stream, but the avalanche speaks,
And their word is louder than freedom, the mountain embrace
Were a death dearer than freedom or freedom's flags.

I will go to the coastline and mingle with men.
These mountain buttresses build beyond the horizon.
They call. But he whom they lay their spell upon
Leaves home, leaves kindred. The range of the telescope's eye
Is well, if the brain follows not to the outermost fields of vision.
I shall drown myself in humanity. Better to lie
Dumb in the city than under the mountainous wavering sky.

The mountains crouch like tigers.
They are but stone yet the seeking eyes grow blind.

## The First Forgotten

*O fons Bandusiae!*
The green hill-orchard where
My great-granduncle lived
Is overgrown. No cache and no reprieve

1

The chilly air holds. They came from the
Old lands, for hunger, or fearing the young
Would shoot from thicket a keeper,
Be transported or hung.

So beholding the strange reeds,
Arrogant flax and fen,
They saw release, eventual and ancestral peace,
Building the stubborn clans again:

Beehives along an elderberry fence . . .
The land is drained. Gorse
Only will grow. To the towns now
Their sons' sons gone, expanding universe:

A light and brittle birth.
I would glorify
Innumerable men in whose breasts my heart once beat,
Is beating. They were slow to die.

One who drove a bullock team
In the gold-rush on an upland track.
One smiling and whistling softly
With a horseshoe behind his back.

Steel mutilates: more, the hollow
Facade, the gaudy mask
On a twisted face. Clay-shut, forgetful, shall
They answer? we ask?

Only the rough and paper bark peeling
From young bluegums, while undergrowth
Among stunted apple-trees coiling
Trips the foot. Sods grass-buried like antique faith.

### High Country Weather

Alone we are born
 And die alone;
Yet see the red-gold cirrus
 Over snow-mountain shine.

Upon the upland road
 Ride easy, stranger:
Surrender to the sky
 Your heart of anger.

## Returned Soldier

The boy who volunteered at seventeen
At twenty-three is heavy on the booze.
Strafed in the desert and bombed out in Crete –
With sore dark eyes and hardened by the heat
Entitled now to call himself a man
And in the doll's-house walk with death at ease:
The Cairo women, cobbers under sand
A death too great for dolls to understand.

Back to a city bed or station hut
At maelstrom centre falling through the night
To dreams where deeper than El Alamein
A buried childhood stirs with leaves and flowers
Remembered girls, the blurred and bitter waters.
Wakes to the midnight rafters and the rain.

## The Bay

On the road to the bay was a lake of rushes
Where we bathed at times and changed in the bamboos.
Now it is rather to stand and say:
How many roads we take that lead to Nowhere,
The alley overgrown, no meaning now but loss:
Not that veritable garden where everything comes easy.

And by the bay itself were cliffs with carved names
And a hut on the shore beside the Maori ovens.
We raced boats from the banks of the pumice creek
Or swam in those autumnal shallows
Growing cold in amber water, riding the logs
Upstream, and waiting for the taniwha.

So now I remember the bay and the little spiders
On driftwood, so poisonous and quick.
The carved cliffs and the great outcrying surf
With currents round the rocks and the birds rising.
A thousand times an hour is torn across
And burned for the sake of going on living.
But I remember the bay that never was
And stand like stone and cannot turn away.

3

## Sea Noon

The grey smoke of rain drifts over headlands
And clear drops fall on the paper as I write.
Only the light thunder and murmur
Of ebbing and flowing furrows is endlessly repeated
And the rapid gulls flash over without sound.

Where is a house with windows open to the afternoon?
With light beer on tables and tobacco smoke
Floating; with a fire in the grate;
With music and the mind-filling pleasure of easy company.
Lying back in a chair to laugh or standing and smiling
One would accept all fates, and even the gold
Melancholy leaves of late autumn
Would seem as natural as a child's toy.

But labour and hunger strides the year
In seasonal repetition, more harsh than tidal waters.
The very rocks are cold: and they were lava once.

So stand the dull green trees bearing the weather
On solitary boughs; so the grey smoke of rain
Drifts on a painted verge of sea and air.
The fisherman casts his net to hold the tide.
Chilly the light wind blowing. And dark the face of noonday
As at the inconsolable parting of friends.

## Elegy for my Father's Father

He knew in the hour he died
That his heart had never spoken
In eighty years of days.
O for the tall tower broken
Memorial is denied:
And the unchanging cairn
That pipes could set ablaze
An aaronsrod and blossom.
They stood by the graveside
From his bitter veins born
And mourned him in their fashion.
A chain of sods in a day
He could slice and build
High as the head of a man
And a flowering cherry tree

4

On his walking shoulder held
Under the lion sun.
When he was old and blind
He sat in a curved chair
All day by the kitchen fire.
Many hours he had seen
The stars in their drunken dancing
Through the burning-glass of his mind
And sober knew the green
Boughs of heaven folding
The winter world in their hand.
The pride of his heart was dumb.
He knew in the hour he died
That his heart had never spoken
In song or bridal bed.
And the naked thought fell back
To a house by the waterside
And the leaves the wind had shaken
Then for a child's sake:
To the waves all night awake
With the dark mouths of the dead.
The tongues of water spoke
And his heart was unafraid.


## Let Time be still

Let Time be still
Who takes all things,
Face, feature, memory
Under his blinding wings.

That I hold again the green
Larch of your body
Whose leaves will gather
The springs of the sky.

And fallen from his cloud
The falcon find
The thigh-encompassed wound
Breasts silken under hand.

Though in a dark room
We knew the day breaking
And the rain-bearing wind
Cold matins making.

5

Sure it seemed
That hidden away
From the sorrowful wind
In deep bracken I lay.

Your mouth was the sun
And green earth under
The rose of your body flowering
Asking and tender
In the timelost season
Of perpetual summer.


## Tunnel Beach

The waist-high sea was rolling
Thunder along her seven iron beaches
As we climbed down to rocks and the curved sand,
Drowned Lyonesse lay lost and tolling
Waiting the cry of the sun's phoenix
From the sea-carved cliffs that held us in their hand.

Forgotten there the green
Paddocks we walked an hour before,
The mare and the foal and the witch-tormented wood
And the flaked salt boughs, for the boughs of flame were seen
Of the first garden and the root
Of graves in your salt mouth and the forehead branded fire.

Through the rock tunnel whined
The wind, Time's hound in leash,
And stirred the sand and murmured in your hair.
The honey of your moving thighs
Drew down the cirrus sky, your doves about the beach
Shut out sea thunder with their wings and stilled the lonely air.

But O rising I heard the loud
Voice of the sea's women riding
All storm to come. No virgin mother bore
My heart wave eaten. From the womb of cloud
Falls now no dove, but combers grinding
Break sullen on the last inviolate shore.

## Haast Pass

In the dense bush all leaves and bark exude
The odour of mortality; for plants
Accept their death like stones
Rooted for ever in time's torrent bed.

Return from here. We have nothing to learn
From the dank falling of fern spores
Or the pure glacier blaze that melts
Down mountains, flowing to the Tasman.

This earth was never ours. Remember
Rather the tired faces in the pub
The children who have never grown. Return
To the near death, the loves like garden flowers.


## To my Father

Today, looking at the flowering peach,
The island off the shore and waves that break
Quiet upon the rocks and level beach –
We must join forces, you and I, remake
The harbour silted and the city bombed
And all our hopes that lie now fire-entombed.

Your country childhood helped to make you strong,
Ploughing at twelve. I only know the man.
While I grew up more sheltered and too long
In love with my disease; though illness can
Impart by dint of pain a different kind
Of toughness to the predatory mind.

There is a feud between us. I have loved
You more than my own good, because you stand
For country pride and gentleness, engraved
In forehead lines, veins swollen on the hand;
Also, behind slow speech and quiet eye
The rock of passionate integrity.

You were a poet whom the time betrayed
To action. So, as Jewish Solomon
Prayed for wisdom, you had prayed
That you might have a poet for a son.
The prayer was answered; but an answer may
Confound by its exactness those who pray.

7

Finding no fault in you, I have been tempted
To stay your child. But that which broke
(Nature) the navel-cord, has not exempted
Even your light and sympathetic yoke.
It is in me your own true mettle shows;
Nor can we thus be friends till we are foes.

This you know well, but it will bear repeating –
Almost you are at times a second self;
Almost at times I feel your heart beating
In my own breast as if there were no gulf
To sever us. And you have seemed then rather
An out-of-time twin brother than a father.

So much is true; yet I have seen the time
When I would cut the past out, like a cancer,
Which now I must digest in awkward rhyme
Until I move 'in measure like a dancer'.
To know an age where all our loves have scope:
It is too much for any man to hope.

You, tickling trout once in a water-race;
You, playing cards, not caring if you lost;
You, shooting hares high on the mountain face;
You, showing me the ferns that grow from frost;
You, quoting Burns and Byron while I listened;
You, breaking quartz until the mica glistened.

These I remember, with the wind that blows
Forever pure down from the tussock ranges;
And these remain, like the everlasting snows,
Changeless in me while my life changes;
These, and a thousand things that prove
You rooted like a tree in the land's love.

I shall compare you to the bended bow,
Myself the arrow launched upon the hollow
Resounding air. And I must go
In time, my friend, to where you cannot follow.
It is not love would hope to keep me young,
The arrow rusted and the bow unstrung.

We have one aim: to set men free
From fear and custom and the incessant war
Of self with self and city against city –
So they may know the peace that they were born for

And find the earth sufficient, who instead
For fruit give scorpions and stones for bread.

And I sit now beside the wishing-well
And drop my silver down. I will have sons
And you grandchildren yet to tell
Old tales despite the anger of the guns:
Leisure to stroll and see Him unafraid
Who walked with Adam once in the green shade.


## Elegy for an Unknown Soldier

There was a time when I would magnify
His ending; scatter words as if I wept
Tears not my own but man's. There was a time.
But not now so. He died of a common sickness.

Nor did any new star shine
Upon that day when he came crying out
Of fleshy darkness to a world of pain
And waxen eyelids let the daylight enter.

So felt and tasted, found earth good enough.
Later he played with stones and wondered
If there was land beyond the dark sea rim
And where the road led out of the farthest paddock.

Awkward at school, he could not master sums.
Could you expect him then to understand
The miracle and menace of his body
That grew as mushrooms grow from dusk to dawn?

He had the weight though for a football scrum
And thought it fine to listen to the cheering
And drink beer with the boys, telling them tall
Stories of girls that he had never known.

So when the War came he was glad and sorry,
But soon enlisted. Then his mother cried
A little, and his father boasted how
He'd let him go, though needed for the farm.

Likely in Egypt he would find out something
About himself, if flies and drunkenness
And deadly heat could tell him much – until
In his first battle a shell splinter caught him.

So crown him with memorial bronze among
The older dead, child of a mountainous island.
Wings of a tarnished victory shadow him
Who born of silence has burned back to silence.

## The Cave

In a hollow of the fields, where one would least expect it,
Stark and suddenly this limestone buttress:
A tree whose roots are bound about the stones,
Broad-leaved, hides well that crevice at the base
That leads, one guesses, to the sunless kingdom
Where souls endure the ache of Proserpine.

Entering where no man it seemed
Had come before, I found a rivulet
Beyond the rock door running in the dark.
Where it sprang from in the heart of the hill
No one could tell: alone
It ran like Time there in the dank silence.

I spoke once and my voice resounded
Among the many pillars. Further in
Were bones of sheep that strayed and died
In nether darkness, brown and water-worn.
The smell of earth was like a secret language
That dead men speak and we have long forgotten.

The whole weight of the hill hung over me.
Gladly I would have stayed there and been hidden
From every beast that moves beneath the sun,
From age's enmity and love's contagion:
But turned and climbed back to the barrier,
Pressed through and came to dazzling daylight out.

## Farmhand

You will see him light a cigarette
At the hall door careless, leaning his back
Against the wall, or telling some new joke
To a friend, or looking out into the secret night.

But always his eyes turn
To the dance floor and the girls drifting like flowers

Before the music that tears
Slowly in his mind an old wound open.

His red sunburnt face and hairy hands
Were not made for dancing or love-making
But rather the earth wave breaking
To the plough, and crops slow-growing as his mind.

He has no girl to run her fingers through
His sandy hair, and giggle at his side
When Sunday couples walk. Instead
He has his awkward hopes, his envious dreams to yarn to.

But ah in harvest watch him
Forking stooks, effortless and strong –
Or listening like a lover to the song
Clear, without fault, of a new tractor engine.

### *Poem by the Clock Tower, Sumner*

Beside the dark sand and the winged foam
Under the shadow of the naked tower
Play the wild children, stranger than Atlanteans.
For them the blazed rock hieroglyph burns clear:
Bear dance and bull dance in the drenched arena
To the sun's trumpet and the waves' crying.

They are the terrible mirrors where our time
Stares back with gorgon eyes. An Ice Age lies
Between us; for they know
The place and hour of the young phoenix' nest
On the bare dune where we can see only
Worn glacial stones and terminal moraine.

And for them rises yet
From earth's still centre the heaven-bearing
Immortal Tree. The ponds and hollow groves
Peopled with fish and speaking birds receive them,
Teach them the language in which stones converse,
Show them the arrows of the toi-toi plume.

We in the murdering city hug our death
Closer than jewels; to the mud-stained sky
Daylong expectant turn one questioning face.
Or in the long night frozen the caress

11

Of flesh on flesh and stone on stone are one
Suspending rainbow in the lost abyss.

Where is the white stone that shall transmute
Our average day to gold?
The green lane that leads to the wishing well
The secret house the fertile wilderness
Where grief and memory are reconciled.
Angels of fire and ice guard well that garden.

And yet the tower stands, four-square and casting
A sundial shadow on the dancing sand.
The blown cloud blares with trumpets. And the wind
Beyond the Cave Rock scatters birds and spume,
Strikes out an echo from the ringing stone,
Strikes where the boat is tugging at its chain.

These images disturb our human night
With joy, and promise of prodigious noon:
Childhood and age in one green cradle joined.
Again from this blind rock of time I know
In heart of lethargy a drowned sun rising;
Again the dark Dove nestles in my breast.


### Virginia Lake

The lake lies blind and glinting in the sun.
Among the reeds the red-billed native birds
Step high like dancers. I have found
A tongue to praise them, who was dumb,
And from the deaf morass one word
Breaks with the voices of the numberless drowned.

This was the garden and the talking water
Where once a child walked and wondered
At the leaves' treasure house, the brown ducks riding
Over the water face, the four winds calling
His name aloud, and a green world under
Where fish like stars in a fallen heaven glided.

And for his love the eyeless statues moved
Down the shell paths. The bandstand set
On fire with music blazing at its centre
Was havened in his love.
The lichened elm was rafters overhead,
Old waves unlocked their gates for him to enter.

Who now lies dumb, the black tongue dry
And the eyes weighed with coins.
O out of this rock tomb
Of labyrinthine grief I start and cry
Toward his real day – the undestroyed
Fantastic Eden of a waking dream.


## Rocket Show

As warm north rain breaks over suburb houses,
Streaming on window glass, its drifting hazes
Covering harbour ranges with a dense hood:
I recall how eighteen months ago I stood
Ankle-deep in sand on an Otago beach
Watching the fireworks flare over strident surf and bach,
In brain grey ash, in heart the sea-change flowing
Of one love dying and another growing.

For love grows like the crocus bulb in winter
Hiding from snow and from itself the tender
Green frond in embryo; but dies as rockets die
(White sparks of pain against a steel-dark sky)
With firebird wings trailing an arc of grief
Across a night inhuman as the grave,
Falling at length a dull and smouldering shell
To frozen dunes and the wash of the quenching swell.

There was little room left where the crowd had trampled
Grass and lupin bare, under the pines that trembled
In gusts from the sea. On a sandhillock I chose
A place to watch from. Then the rockets rose,
O marvellous, like self-destroying flowers
On slender stems, with seed-pods full of flares,
Raining down amber, scarlet, pennies from heaven
On the skyward straining heads and still sea-haven.
Had they brought death, we would have stood the same,
I think, in ecstasy at the world-end flame.

It is the rain streaming reminds me of
Those ardent showers, cathartic love and grief.
As I walked home through the cold streets by moonlight,
My steps ringing in the October night,
I thought of our strange lives, the grinding cycle
Of death and renewal come to full circle,
And of man's heart, that blind Rosetta stone,
Mad as the polar moon, decipherable by none.

## Wild Bees

Often in summer, on a tarred bridge plank standing,
Or downstream between willows, a safe Ophelia drifting
In a rented boat – I had seen them come and go,
Those wild bees swift as tigers, their gauze wings a-glitter
In passionless industry, clustering black at the crevice
Of a rotten cabbage tree, where their hive was hidden low.

But never strolled too near. Till one half-cloudy evening
Of ripe January, my friends and I
Came, gloved and masked to the eyes like plundering
        desperadoes,
To smoke them out. Quiet beside the stagnant river
We trod wet grasses down, hearing the crickets chitter
And waiting for light to drain from the wounded sky.

Before we reached the hive their sentries saw us
And sprang invisible through the darkening air,
Stabbed, and died in stinging. The hive woke. Poisonous fuming
Of sulphur filled the hollow trunk, and crawling
Blue flame sputtered – yet still their suicidal
Live raiders dived and clung to our hands and hair.

O it was Carthage under the Roman torches,
Or loud with flames and falling timber, Troy!
A job well botched. Half of the honey melted
And half the rest young grubs. Through earth-black
        smouldering ashes
And maimed bees groaning, we drew out our plunder.
Little enough their gold, and slight our joy.

Fallen then the city of instinctive wisdom.
Tragedy is written distinct and small:
A hive burned on a cool night in summer.
But loss is a precious stone to me, a nectar
Distilled in time, preaching the truth of winter
To the fallen heart that does not cease to fall.


## The Morgue

Each morning when I lit the coke furnace
Unwillingly I passed the locked door,
The room where Death lived. Shadowless infection
Looked from the blind panes, and an open secret

14

Stained even the red flowers in the rock garden
Flesh-fingered under the sanatorium wall.

And each day the patients coming and going
From light jobs, joking below the sombre pines,
Would pass without looking, their faces leaner
As if the wintry neighbourhood of Death
Would strip the shuddering flesh from bone. They shouted,
Threw clods at one another, and passed on.

But when at length, with stiff broom and bucket,
I opened the door wide – well, there was nothing
To fear. Only the bare close concrete wall,
A slab of stone, and a wheeled canvas stretcher.
For Death had shifted house to his true home
And mansion, ruinous, of the human heart.

## Poem in the Matukituki Valley

Some few yards from the hut the standing beeches
Let fall their dead limbs, overgrown
With feathered moss and filigree of bracken.
The rotted wood splits clean and hard
Close-grained to the driven axe, with sound of water
Sibilant falling and high nested birds.

In winter blind with snow; but in full summer
The forest blanket sheds its cloudy pollen
And cloaks a range in undevouring fire.
Remote the land's heart. Though the wild scrub cattle
Acclimatized, may learn
Shreds of her purpose, or the taloned kea.

For those who come as I do, half-aware,
Wading the swollen
Matukituki waist-high in snow water,
And stumbling where the mountains throw their dice
Of boulders huge as houses, or the smoking
Cataract flings its arrows on our path –

For us the land is matrix and destroyer,
Resentful, darkly known
By sunset omens, low words heard in branches;
Or where the red deer lift their innocent heads
Snuffing the wind for danger,
And from our footfall's menace bound in terror.

Three emblems of the heart I carry folded
As charms against flood water, sliding shale:
Pale gentian, lily, and bush orchid.
The peaks too have names to suit their whiteness,
Stargazer and Moonraker,
A sailor's language and a mountaineer's.

And those who sleep in close bags fitfully
Besieged by wind in a snowline bivouac –
The carrion parrot with red underwing
Clangs on the roof by night, and daybreak brings
Raincloud on purple ranges, light reflected
Stainless from crumbling glacier, dazzling snow,

Do they not, clay in that unearthly furnace,
Endure the hermit's peace
And mindless ecstasy? Blue-lipped crevasse
And smooth rock chimney straddling – a communion
With what eludes our net – Leviathan
Stirring to ocean birth our inland waters?

Sky's purity; the altar cloth of snow
On deathly summits laid; or avalanche
That shakes the rough moraine with giant laughter;
Snowplume and whirlwind – what are these
But His flawed mirror who gave the mountain strength
And dwells in holy calm, undying freshness?

Therefore we turn, hiding our souls' dullness
From that too blinding glass: turn to the gentle
Dark of the human daydream, child and wife,
Patience of stone and soil, the lawful city
Where man may live, and no wild trespass
Of what's eternal shake his grave of time.


## Thoughts of a Dying Calvinist

The night's foul with hail and sleet
As I lie cold in linen sheet
And sweat long but get no heat.
*The fear of death confounds me.*

I could lie ill though happ'd in clay,
For there in Crookieden they say
The fire eats flesh and soul away.
*The fear of death confounds me.*

16

A brief thirst that none can slake,
A brief word, a brief wake,
A brief road that all must take –
*The fear of death confounds me.*

About the bed my kindred cry;
The greedy gled has a moister eye.
Deil take their carrion hearts to fry!
*The fear of death confounds me.*

When Brother John the Elder died
They broke the housewall open wide
To get his glutton's corpse outside.
*The fear of death confounds me.*

The wedding guests their meal begin,
But the ghost that dies in deadly sin
Shall knock but never enter in.
*The fear of death confounds me.*

O thou my God, judge as thou art,
Conning each man's black-rotten heart,
Take thou this hour the sinner's part.
*The fear of death confounds me.*

And bid me, Andrew Crummock, rise
To see thy Face in paradise
Or sleep now with the beast that dies.
*The fear of death confounds me.*


## *The Fallen House*

I took the clay track leading
From Black Bridge to Duffy's farm,
In no forefarer's footmark treading,
Thus free, it would seem, from any harm
That could befall me – the kind of ill-luck charm
That clings to a once-fair steading –

When South the sky thickened
And rain came pelter on the hill-scurf:
So in a grove (where the wind quickened
Their young leaves like the mile-off surf)
Of gums I sheltered, whose roots had drained the turf
Of life till a starved soil sickened.

But an older grief spoke plainly
From the green mound where thistle strewed
Her bearded gossamer. Ungainly
The sprawled stones fire-blackened could
Recall man; though where the house stood
Stands ragged thistle only.

It was not Woe that flaunted
Funereal plume and banner there,
Nor an Atridean doom that daunted
The heart with a lidless gorgon stare;
But darker the cradling bluegums, sombre the air,
By the wraith of dead joy haunted.

There once the murk was cloven
By hearthlight fondly flaring within:
Adamant seemed their hope and haven.
O Time, Time takes in a gin
The quick of being! Pale now and gossamer-thin
The web their lives had woven.

### Tarras Moon

When Tim and I stumbled
On the rough Tarras track
(We shared the station shack)
Blind drunk we fumbled
Like ferrets in a sack
Together tumbled,
*That no way can fare.*

I knew her not from a lantern
Or a lowe in the lift –
Grim in her graveshift
The bare poxy wanton,
Queen Death glowered from a rift
Of cloudwrack above the mountain,
*Walking on wild air.*

'Ripe archaic' her feature
From a Sicilian metope,
Two snakes for a knotted rope
About her middle: the creature
That eats our carrion hope:
Glass of malignant Nature,
*Diana chastely fair.*

'She's like my granny, but older
By a long chalk,' Tim said.
In a corpselight hither shed
Clear shone tussock and boulder:
Like men already dead
Under Mt Iron's shoulder
*Moonstruck we staggered there.*


## Book of the Dead

Pollen-heavy the black bee
Above the flaring clematis drones;
Fennel and flax among the gravestones
Flourish, and rough cabbage-tree.
  *Stranger, of your charity*
  *Pray for the souls*
  *Of those hereunder*
  *That they in light perpetual tarry.*

'A bushman I; so rejoiced
When roots of laurel burst apart
Angel and cross, drove through my heart,
And the night grass murmured million-voiced.'
  *Stranger, of your charity*
  *Pray for the soul*
  *Of Harry Garnett*
  *That he in light perpetual tarry.*

'Dad thrashed me till I thrashed Dad.
At twenty-four an A.B.
A knife in the back at a mollhouse spree,
And my long home was the first I had.'
  *Stranger, of your charity*
  *Pray for the soul*
  *Of Nathan Carpenter*
  *That he in light perpetual tarry.*

'Loth was I to leave earth,
The house built newly, the gully farm
With my dear love ploughing; but beyond harm
The bones that proved too small for childbirth.'
  *Stranger, of your charity*
  *Pray for the soul*
  *Of Mary Hamilton*
  *That she in light perpetual tarry.*

19

'Din of no upland watercourse
Fills my dead ear; but the low sound
I heard as a lad from springs profound
That eddy at the Severn's source.'
    *Stranger, of your charity*
    *Pray for the soul*
    *Of John Trevellyan*
    *That he in light perpetual tarry.*

'A down-at-heel remittance man
From a good home; but better, this.
Friend, fare on. My tipple is
Not brandy but oblivion.'
    *Stranger, of your charity*
    *Pray for the soul*
    *Of Hugh Beaumont*
    *That he in light perpetual tarry.*

Not fifty yards from college and shop
Lie they, long ensepulchred.
Her wild wing earthward bending, a bird
Pecks for seed on the fennel top.
    *Stranger, of your charity*
    *Pray for the souls*
    *Of these hereunder*
    *That they in light perpetual tarry.*


## The Homecoming

Odysseus has come home, to the gully farm
Where the macrocarpa windbreak shields a house
Heavy with time's reliques – the brown-filmed photographs
Of ghosts more real than he; the mankind-measuring arm
Of a pendulum clock; and true yet to her vows,
His mother, grief's Penelope. At the blind the sea wind laughs.

The siege more long and terrible than Troy's
Begins again. A love demanding all,
Hypochondriacal, sea-dark and contentless:
This was the sour ground that nurtured a boy's
Dream of freedom; this, in Circe's hall
Drugged him; his homecoming finds this, more relentless.

She does not say, 'You have changed'; nor could she imagine any
Otherwise to the quiet maelstrom spinning
In the circle of their days. Still she would wish to carry

Him folded within her, shut from the wild and many
Voices of life's combat, in the cage of beginning;
She counts it natural that he should never marry.

She will cook his meals; complain of the south weather
That wrings her joints. And he – rebels; and yields
To the old covenant – calms the bleating
Ewe in birth travail. The smell of saddle leather
His sacrament; or the sale day drink; yet hears beyond sparse fields
On reef and cave the sea's hexameter beating.

## Never No More

Oh the summer's afloat on spindrift beaches
Brown as bread in a holiday heaven:
The same sweet lie the lupin teaches
As always dropping her gay pollen
On a girl's print frock leg shoulder bare
*Never no more never no more.*

The boys climb to their branch-high houses
Under a black bridge dive for pennies
The noon cloud like a bird's breast downy
Night come cool as a hawthorn berry
Kite tails tied on a telephone wire
*Never no more never no more.*

Cigarette stink from a hole in the rushes
Dark as a dunny the under-runner
The green flax plaited for whiplashes
Cockabully finned with the fire of summer
*Jack loves Jill* on the garage door
*Never no more never no more.*

The trodden path in the brambles led
Sweet and sure to a lifted frock
To the boathouse spree and the hayloft bed
A hamstrung heart and no way back:
Like a toi-toi arrow shot in the air
*Never no more never no more.*

21

## The Surfman's Story

On such a day as this
When breakers bay on the reef like a minutegun
    Or up the tall beach grind and hiss
    Like flattened snakes – we hauled out
    Tackle and lifeline, at the run,
For two swept seaward, bathers, caught in the current's rout.

    (There by the Maori Rock
A narrow rip runs out, rapid as death,
    Each tide, regular as the clock:
    Nothing to fear, once known – but a few
    Fool bathers drowned there a bad name bequeath
Till it grows to a gorgon myth, a cud for gossips to chew.)

    I stood by the reel
And Jake plunged in a smother of surf and sand.
    He could swim, that boy, like a river-eel;
    It was hard going even for his crawlstroke –
    I cursed the mad bathers, you'll understand.
Over his head the flurry of waves battered and broke.

    He told us after how
They beat him off; or rather the man did (she
    Was near sinking). He warded the blow,
    Trod water, waited; then by the hair
    Hauled her, a dead weight, from the treacherous sea
Back through the hurly-burly of breakers to earth and air.

    We worked for an hour to keep
The spark in her body alive; then gave her rum,
    Wrapt her in blankets to lie and sleep
    In the shed down there (the lupin and swordgrass
    Half hide it). But when she had come
To her senses it was only to yammer and cry *Alas*.

    Like a dove that has lost its mate,
Or an eagle maybe (she had more that look
    In the full lip and nose knife-straight,
    Great cavernous eye): she'd have run back
    To the brawling sea if I hadn't took
Her by the arms and held her – the bruises stayed blue-black.

It seemed they had made a pact
To drown together, impatient of Love's slow
  Guttering to death, and what life lacked
  For two fettered in wedlock, wild
  To wound each other – the undertow
Of passion drew them till it seemed the blind sea smiled.

  Well – he was washed ashore
Some weeks after, eaten by fishes, foul
  With tangleweed. She cried no more.
  We were married within the year: that house
  By the river's ours, with the climbing cowl
Of woodsmoke, the paddock behind, in a nest of orchard boughs.


## The Journey

  Then, coming to the long ship, they stowed
Wineskins aboard, water from the sedgy creek,
  With red apples, honey from the wild bees' hoard
  By shepherds ransacked from a ravens' cleft
  Where ivies tomb the twilight and the spider keeps
Vigil yearlong. All these, gifts of the goddess, were lashed
Under the rowers' benches – the bellowing ram also
And black ewe, on whose fleece the flung saltflake dries.

  With handclasp, singing, and shed tears they take
Leave of Aeaea, the green isle summer-browed,
  Isle of their drowsy feasting. With the sound of *never,*
  The keel rasped on sand, rode, rocked on the greymaned wave.
  Moaning and manybreasted, the whale's path lay
Westward, perilous, to Cimmeria the sunless
And Hades' silence. All eyes looked back.
Only Odysseus, in the ship's prow standing, did not turn or speak.

  And like a stormbird through daylight and darkness
She fled, a serpent wake behind her coiling,
  The sun a brazen shield, or clammy nightfogs drifting,
  Till at the frontiers of the murmuring Dead
  They beached, where poplar and lamenting willow
Let fall their vacant seed. There made
Sacrifice to Persephone, sprinkled the white barley.
The Dead gathered, like moths, with wrath and ululation.

## Seraphion

I, Seraphion, hermit of Mount Athos,
Three hundred feet above the sea's mumble
Alone in a rock shelter, the sparrow's refuge
With a stone couch, one ikon and a lamp,
In the judgement of the eye of absolute Day
Await the hour of my death.

I, Seraphion, was once Demetrios
Singer of ballads, thief and actor.
Lord, let these swollen joints, back bruised by the scourge,
Eyes weak with tears and icy fasting,
Be acceptable sacrifice, sign of the penitent – Deliver,
O Lord, my soul alive!

This voice, whose psalms startle the gull, once
In wineshops won silver and applause; these knees, that bend
Hourly, in the pit of perfumed beds
Opened the thighs of harlots. In Alexandrian gardens,
In the brothels of Beirut, in the mire of Babylon
My invisible Enemy triumphed and trod me down.

Till in black night came One, the Shepherd, to wash me
Clean of the burning raddle. Let Him be praised:
With Him alone is power. I woke and fled
To the rock of Athos, shunning
All temporal beauty, solace of wall and vineyard
To praise Him in the desert of His Truth.

On Athos is no sight or sound of woman,
No female thing, no, not a pigeon cloistered
On monastery roofs. In this bare place
My hermitage, I see only at evening
The face of him who brings me water and lentils,
Kneels for my blessing, and goes, with no word said.

But at night a voice comes on the wind, a phantom
Torments me, touching my ageing limbs with fire:
A sea boy out of Smyrna. Two years we lived
In unlawful love, thieving and drinking together,
Till he left me for a wealthy Lebanese
For a new overcoat and a villa in Cairo.

24

With mouth of pomegranate, with skin of jessamine,
With eyes like wintry flowers, with cheeks firm as olives,
With corrupt blood, with the treachery of a panther.
Two years we lived at loggerheads together.
In his flesh I embraced the flesh of the young Hyakinthos,
And between midnight and morning he taunts me still.

## Perseus

Leaving them, children of the Sun, to their perpetual
Unwearying dance about the ancient Tree,
Perseus flew east, the bird-winged sandals beating
Smooth and monotonous; sauntered above
Fens peopled by the placid watersnake,
Flamingo, crocodile –

And those unfallen creatures, joyful in
Their maze of waters, watched; with reedy voices
Praised the oncoming hero; cried
And coupled in his path. But he felt only
Scorching his shoulders, the shield, Athene's lovegift –
    and the first
Wind of foreboding blow from Medusa's home.

So entered the stone kingdom where no life
Startled, but brackish water fell
Like tears from solitary beds
Of spaghnum moss, or spray from cataracts
Sprinkled the grey-belled orchid, feathered grass
And spider's coverlet.

Till by the final cleft precipitous
At a blind gorge's end he lighted, stood,
Unslung the heavy shield, drew breath, and waited
As the bright hornet waits and quivers
Hearing within her den the poisonous rustle
And mew, for battle angry, of tarantula.

Fair smote her face upon the burning shield,
Medusa, image of the soul's despair,
Snake-garlanded, child of derisive Chaos
And hateful Night, whom no man may
Look on and live. In horror, pity, loathing,
Perseus looked long, lifted his sword, and struck.

Then empty was the cave. A vulture's taloned body
Headless and huddled, a woman's marble face
With snakes for hair – and in the wide
Thoroughfares of the sky no hint of cloudy fury
Or clanging dread, as homeward he
Trod, the pouched Despair at his girdle hanging,

To earth, Andromeda, the palace garden
His parents bickered in, plainsong of harvest –
To the lawgiver's boredom, rendering
(The task accomplished) back to benignant Hermes
And holy Athene goods not his own, the borrowed
Sandals of courage and the shield of art.

## Jack the Swagger's Song

'Damn this dry shingle country,'
Old Jack the swagger cried –
'The rutting hare beneath; above
The brown hawk in his pride;
And not one green gooseberry bush
To suck and lay beside.

'Beyond the Rock and Pillar
One day when I was young
I plucked a berry from the bush
And laid it on my tongue:
No sourer, wilder, gladder fruit
From the grey schist rock sprung.

'Ten feet below the creekbed
Those buried waters lie,
And had I but one billy full
I'd mock the raging sky –
But crazy in the heat mirage
Like any beast I'll die;

'And when the squatter hears it
At most he'll thumb his reins
And say, "Bad Luck!" – and soon the creek
(From an icefield it drains)
Headhigh will soak my shirt and run
Aflood in my dry veins.'

## Elegy at the Year's End

At the year's end I come to my father's house
Where passion fruit hang gold above an open doorway
And garden trees bend to the visiting bird:
   Here first the single vision
Entered my heart, as to a dusty room
Enters the pure tyrannical wind of heaven.

The coal burns out; the quiet ash remains
That tired minds and coarsened bodies know.
   Small town of corrugated iron roofs
Between the low volcanic saddle
And offshore reef where blue cod browse,
From husks of exile, humbled, I come to your fond prison.

At an elder uncle's deathbed I read the graph
Of suffering in the face of country cousins.
   These have endured what men hold in common,
The cross of custom, the marriage bed of knives;
Their angular faces reflecting his
Whose body lies stiff under the coverlet.

One may walk again to the fisherman's rock, hearing
The long waves tumble, from America riding
Where mottled kelpbeds heave to a pale sun,
   But not again see green Aphrodite
Rise to transfigure the noon. Rather the Sophoclean
Chorus: *All shall be taken.*

Or by the brown lagoon stand idle
Where to their haunted coves the safe flocks go,
And envy the paradise drake his brilliant sexual plumage.
   For single vision dies. Spirit and flesh are sundered
In the kingdom of no love. Our stunted passions bend
To serve again familiar social devils.

Brief is the visiting angel. In corridors of hunger
Our lives entwined suffer the common ill:
Living and dying, breathing and begetting.
Meanwhile on maimed gravestones under the towering fennel
Moves the bright lizard, sunloved, basking in
   The moment of animal joy.

# Lament for Barney Flanagan

## Licensee of the Hesperus Hotel

Flanagan got up on a Saturday morning,
Pulled on his pants while the coffee was warming;
He didn't remember the doctor's warning,
　'Your heart's too big, Mr Flanagan.'

Barney Flanagan, sprung like a frog
From a wet root in an Irish bog –
May his soul escape from the tooth of the dog!
　God have mercy on Flanagan.

Barney Flanagan R.I.P.
Rode to his grave on Hennessy's
Like a bottle-cork boat in the Irish Sea.
　The bell-boy rings for Flanagan.

Barney Flanagan, ripe for a coffin,
Eighteen stone and brandy-rotten,
Patted the housemaid's velvet bottom –
　'Oh, is it you, Mr Flanagan?'

The sky was bright as a new milk token.
Bill the Bookie and Shellshock Hogan
Waited outside for the pub to open –
　'Good day, Mr Flanagan.'

At noon he was drinking in the lounge bar corner
With a sergeant of police and a racehorse owner
When the Angel of Death looked over his shoulder –
　'Could you spare a moment, Flanagan?'

Oh the deck was cut; the bets were laid;
But the very last card that Barney played
Was the Deadman's Trump, the bullet of Spades –
　'Would you like more air, Mr Flanagan?'

The priest came running but the priest came late
For Barney was banging at the Pearly Gate.
St Peter said, 'Quiet! You'll have to wait
　For a hundred masses, Flanagan.'

The regular boys and the loud accountants
Left their nips and their seven-ounces
As chickens fly when the buzzard pounces –
　'Have you heard about old Flanagan?'

28

Cold in the parlour Flanagan lay
Like a bride at the end of her marriage day.
The Waterside Workers' Band will play
   A brass goodbye to Flanagan.

While publicans drink their profits still,
While lawyers flock to be in at the kill,
While Aussie barmen milk the till
   We will remember Flanagan.

For Barney had a send-off and no mistake.
He died like a man for his country's sake;
And the Governor-General came to his wake.
   Drink again to Flanagan!

*Despise not, O Lord, the work of Thine own hands*
*And let light perpetual shine upon him.*


## The Giant's Grave

Some heavens ago, when the wind blew from a calmer
Airt, and stood yet Atlas, benignant Titan,
At the winged horizon's gate, his locks of cloud unshorn,
Heaving the sky on his shoulders – there deep in memory's glass,
Free of the torturer's hand, I and my elder brother
Walk the green riverbank in the land where I was born.

On one side, high ground ridged by cattletracks
Where our careering sledges would often whip from grassheads,
Before sunrise, a soaking dew; the beer-brown somnolent wave
Of the brackish river, cattleflats beyond it,
Brimmed sluggish under gorsepods; between them, a narrow
   tumulus,
Manuka-groved, broom-feathered, we called *The Giant's Grave*.

The horned beasts roared, ponderous at their crossing,
Dewlap-plunged in the dark stream; all night the reedy voices
Cried, *Aqua! Aqua!*, breaking the skin of sleep,
From ditch and bog; at noon the swampgrass flared
Smoke-pillared sacrifice, burned back to a stump of ashes
Beside Antaeus' bones in the grave-mound bedded deep.

In its rock flank a ngaio tree gave foothold,
Flesh-leaved, whose tarry buds breaking in flower sprinkled
Dust on an ageless mirror. There my brother laid
Lines for the basking eels, brutes thicker than a forearm,

29

Sailed his flaxstick navy, twig-masted on rough ripples
Flogged by desire's crosswind. Nothing made us afraid.

No, not fear of drowning, drawn down in weedy arms,
Nor any ghost dragging the eyes unwilling
To gaze on Adam's wound. Yet once, in a safe bed,
Sweating, chilled by nightmare, I saw a pyre kindled
On the river mound, and stark there, her face in anguish smiling,
Ablaze and unconsumed, my loved grandmother, dead.

## The Rock Woman

Here the south sea washes
Kelpbed and margin of the drumhard sand.
Its grey surf-pillars thundering
Concede no altar, no denial
But an obscure torment
At the mind's edge trembling, about to be.

Continually, as a boy, I came to this
Rock ledge above the sinuous wave
Where dogs and gulls left excrement,
As if the sea-split ground could set at ease
The wish to be no longer man
That wrenched me then, that overstrides me now.

A rock carved like a woman,
Pain's torso, guardian of the place,
Told raining beads. I did not know
What grief her look wrung dry,
In what blind rooms and tombs
I and my fellows would walk heavily.

Magdalen of the rock
Unvirgin pray for us.
In the wave's throb our agonies awake
Rise to your true-all-suffering kiss.
In hewn rock of prayer
You ask for us the death hour's peace.

## Heard in a Sod Chimney

'What eye could wish for more,'
    Sings the first voice in the wind,
'Than yellow spume on the seashore,

30

Glitter of breakers boiling,
And a girl wading there
Whom the hard light strips,
Breast and hips, grey eyes, and brindled hair
A nest of young snakes coiling?'

'Ah, no such countenance,'
  Sings the second voice in the wind,
'But the town girl at a country dance
A swan among geese sailing
(How they cackle and hiss!) –
Her high heels clattering go
To and fro: no farmer's son dare kiss
That proud mouth at the frostwhite railing.'

'How bright the marsh fires burn!'
  Sings the third voice in the wind.
'I have blown over many a cairn
And bone to bone spieling
Had heavy tales to tell
How this one, that one, fair
In the world's air drew breath and glimmered well
Who now stares blind at a marble ceiling.'


### The Fisherman

Between the day and evening
I fish from Barney's rock,
And watch the weedy channels fill
And hear the small waves knock,
And feel below their ledge's roof
The tugging greenbone flock.

When spiring seabirds mingle
Between the wave and sky,
The ka'wai chase the herrings in
Like soldiers dressed to die,
And on the beach for hands to pick
In flapping shoals they lie.

Upon an army pension
It suits a single man
To take from the sea's full cupboard
Whatever food he can.
The wound I got at Passchendaele
Throbs with the dying sun.

While loud across the sandhills
Clangs out the Sunday bell
I drop my line and sinker down
Through the weed-fronded swell,
And what I see there after dark
Let the blind wave tell.


## Crossing Cook Strait

The night was clear, sea calm; I came on deck
To stretch my legs, find perhaps
Gossip, a girl in green slacks at the rail
Or just the logline feathering a dumb wake.

The ship swung in the elbow of the Strait.
'Dolphins!' I cried – 'let the true sad Venus
Rise riding her shoals, teach me as once to wonder
And wander at ease, be glad and never regret.'

But night increased under the signal stars.
In the dark bows, facing the flat sea,
Stood one I had not expected, yet knew without surprise
As the Janus made formidable by loveless years.

His coat military; his gesture mild –
'Well met,' he said, 'on the terrestrial journey
From chaos into light – what light it is
Contains our peril and purpose, history has not revealed.'

'Sir –', I began. He spoke with words of steel –
'I am Seddon and Savage, the socialist father.
You have known me only in my mask of Dionysus
Amputated in bar rooms, dismembered among wheels.

'I woke in my civil tomb hearing a shout
For bread and justice. It was not here.
That sound came thinly over the waves from China;
Stones piled on my grave had all but shut it out.

'I walked forth gladly to find the angry poor
Who are my nation; discovered instead
The glutton seagulls squabbling over crusts
And policies made and broken behind locked doors.

'I have watched the poets also at their trade.
I have seen them burning with a wormwood brilliance.
Love was the one thing lacking on their page,
The crushed herb of grief at another's pain.

'Your civil calm breeds inward poverty
That chafes for change. The ghost of Adam
Gibbering demoniac in drawing-rooms
Will drink down hemlock with his sugared tea.

'You feed your paupers concrete. They work well,
Ask for no second meal, vote, pay tribute
Of silence on Anzac Day in the pub urinal;
Expose death only by a mushroom smell.

'My counsel was naïve. Anger is bread
To the poor, their guns more accurate than justice,
Because their love has not decayed to a wintry fungus
And hope to the wish for power among the dead.

'In Kaitangata the miner's falling sweat
Wakes in the coal seam fossil flowers.
The clerk puts down his pen and takes his coat;
He will not be back today or the next day either.'

With an ambiguous salute he left me.
The ship moved into a stronger sea,
Bludgeoned alive by the rough mystery
Of love in the running straits of history.


## A Rope for Harry Fat

Oh some have killed in angry love
    And some have killed in hate,
And some have killed in foreign lands
    To serve the business State.
The hangman's hands are abstract hands
    Though sudden death they bring –
'The hangman keeps our country pure,'
    Says Harry Fat the King.

Young love will kick the chairs about
    And like a rush fire burn,
Desiring what it cannot have,
    A true love in return.
Who knows what rage and darkness fall

33

When lovers' thoughts grow cold?
'Whoever kills must pay the price,'
  Says Harry Fat the old.

With violent hands a young man tries
  To mend the shape of life.
This one used a shotgun
  And that one used a knife.
And who can see the issues plain
  That vex our groaning dust?
'The Law is greater than the man,'
  Says Harry Fat the just.

Te Whiu was too young to vote,
  The prison records show.
Some thought he was too young to hang;
  Legality said, *No.*
Who knows what fear the raupo hides
  Or where the wild duck flies?
'A trapdoor and a rope is best,'
  Says Harry Fat the wise.

Though many a time he rolled his coat
  And on the bare boards lay,
He lies in heavy concrete now
  Until the Reckoning Day.
In linen sheet or granite aisle
  Sleep Ministers of State.
'We cannot help the idle poor,'
  Says Harry Fat the great.

Mercy stirred like a summer wind
  The wigs and polished boots
And the long Jehovah faces
  Above their Sunday suits.
The jury was uncertain;
  The judge debated long.
'Let Justice take her rightful course,'
  Said Harry Fat the strong.

The butcher boy and baker boy
  Were whistling in the street
When the hangman bound Te Whiu's eyes
  And strapped his hands and feet,
Who stole to buy a bicycle
  And killed in panic blood.

'The parson won his soul at length,'
   Said Harry Fat the good.

Oh some will kill in rage and fear
   And some will kill in hate,
And some will kill in foreign lands
   To serve the master State.
Justice walks heavy in the land;
   She bears a rope and shroud.
'We will not change our policy,'
   Says Harry Fat the proud.


## At Hokianga

Green floating mangrove pods reveal,
Plucked from the lagging tide, their small
Man-in-a-boat, kernel and clitoris:
Set free to sail, they climb a hundred beaches,
Germinate in night-black mud. Tell,
Historian, how the broken tribes were healed
In a land of exhausted wells, north
From that great ragged capital
Flung like a coat to rot on garden earth.

In houses thatched with nikau palm,
Fearing the dead, riding bareback
On hill stallions, those who learned before us
The secret of survival, to be patient,
Suffer, and shut no doors,
Change all things to their habit, bridge
The bogs with branch laid to branch:
Nourished at compliant breasts, wish only
To drink with friends, own a launch.

To scrape the bones of the dead, how needful,
Lest they should walk, undo forgetfulness
With blight on crops, sickness at home.
In packed ground the missionary fathers
Drowned at river crossings, rest in one bed,
While a boy cuts from flax a spirit boat
Perfect, lightly as a bird's wing
Riding the void of waters
Untaught, a full hour floating.

## At Akitio

Consider this barbarian coast,
Traveller, you who have lost
Lover or friend. It has never made
Anything out of anything.
Drink at these bitter springs.

Fishing at river mouth, a woman
Uses the sea-drilled stone her mother used
For sinker, as big kahawai come,
As tides press upward to time's source.
This coast is shelter to the shearing gangs
Who burn dead matai in their kitchen.

Squirearch, straight-backed rider, built
An ethos of the leisured life,
Lawn, antlered hall and billiard room,
Glass candelabra brought from Paris,
The homestead foundered among fields.
Unhorsed they sleep.

A girl with a necklace of mako teeth
They dug from a sandcliff facing south,
Axe and broken needle.
Stay good under slab and cross
Thin bones of children burnt by cholera,
Made tidy by the last strict nurse.
As tributary of a greater stream
Your single grief enlarges now
The voice of night in kumara gardens,
Prayer of the bush pigeon.

One drowned at the cattle crossing,
One tossed and kicked by a bucking horse –
Who died without confession, wanting
No wafer in their teeth –
Does the toi-toi plume their altar?
Are they held safe in the sea's grail?
This gullied mounded earth, tonned
With silence, and the sun's gaze
On a choir of breakers, has outgrown
The pain of love. Drink,
Traveller, at these pure springs.

Remember, though, the early strength
Of bull-voiced water when the boom broke
And eels clung to the banks, logs
Plunged and pierced the river hymen.
Remember iron-coloured skulls
Of cattle thrown to the crab's crypt,
Driftwood piled by river flood
On the long beach, battered limb
And loin where the red-backed spider breeds,
By a halcyon sea the shapes of man,
Emblems of our short fever.

Pluck then from ledges of the sea
Crayfish for the sack. Not now but later
Think what you were born for. Drink,
Child, at the springs of sleep.

## Howrah Bridge

*(to my wife)*

Taller than the stair of Qtub Minar
These iron beams oppress the eagle's town.
Bare heels will dint them slowly.
And swollen Gunga's muscles move
Beneath, with freight of garbage,
Oar and sail, the loot of many lives.

In the unsleeping night my thoughts
Are millet falling from an iron pan,
While you, my dear, in Delhi lying down
Enter the same room by another door.
The rupee god has trampled here;
The poor implore a Marxist cage.
Dragon seed, the huddled bundles lying
In doorways have perhaps one chilli,
A handful of ground maize.
King Famine rules. Tout and owl-eyed whore
Whose talons pluck and stain the sleeve,
Angels of judgement, husk the soul
Till pity, pity only stays.

*Out of my wounds they have made stars:*
*Each is an eye that looks on you.*

37

## Eioko

That one should suffer for a nation,
Small folded hands, blackcurrant eyes
Alive with character among the sequins:
Eioko, sold in Choshi by her father
(Leg sores and all) for thirty thousand yen,
As if with stakes of split bamboo
To bank one paddy field against the river.

*Her templebones pierced for the blood to flow*
*Lest she should die untimely*
(By God transfusèd thence to graceless souls)
*Eight days head down above a charcoal pit . . .*
For Eioko, a deadlier martyrdom,
At drunken midnight tables
Displayed like butcher's meat, unable
To yawn at will, or smoke or frown or sit,

Becomes a stupid mask, an aching cistern.

The granite maxim: One must always please
Tourist, soldier, ape and boor,
With courtesy more durable than love.
Great dolls like captives nod above her bed.
In Tokyo's ashy dawn she gently touches
A chopstick-holder carved like a green fish,
Sharing her rice bowl with a child more poor.


## At the Tomb of Theseus

Bramble and couchgrass twine above
The tumulus of giant bones.
This king despised his mother's love,
Subdued bullheaded chaos, built
An aqueduct, a cenotaph.
His bones rot like other bones.
Human hatred, human guilt,
Fuel the engine of the State.
The legless beggar at the gate
Has freedom still to spit and laugh.
The twining couchgrass seeds above
Bones that were ignorant of love.

## Be Happy in Bed

One landscape, many women:
Ambition of that savage empty boy
Haunting the bathing sheds and diamond bay,
Composing verses in an upstairs room.
Now the long windings of a broken sense
In humorous elegiacs write his doom.

Boathouses on the edge of Nowhere
Recur to trouble after-dinner sleep,
White legs among the cords and rowlocks –
'There is a spirit in the moving water
Forgives and understands us
Though God has gone inside and slammed the door.'
Where the boats ride endlessly
Grip and hold the sea king's daughter.

Sex taught him sadness: like St Lawrence
Roasting on the grid of conscience:
'One side is brown; now try the other.'
The self so persecuted by enigmas
Prefers a mountain to a nagging mother.

Put off the past: you have endured it,
Enjoyed, or else confessed it.
This luxury like cut veins in a bath
Stains too much the moving water.
No meaning now in that direction
Though skeletons toward the salt pans creep.
The age of sex, the age of centaurs
Returns to punish after-dinner sleep.


## Mandrakes for Supper

Memory feeds us on a prison diet
Of bits and scraps. 'Remember Mr X –,
That simple solemn man, so deathly quiet;

'And Sally Z –, compounded of raw sex
And circumstance' – 'Ah yes, her corn-gold hair . . .'
A land where roams Tyrannosaurus Rex,

The giant lizard, calloused by despair –
In Nowhere I received my education
(If memory can be trusted) mooching there

39

Like Dante's ghost, among a faceless nation.
The white antarctic Gorgon was my mentor:
Her cloudy arms, her eyes of desolation

Sisterly gazing from the whirlwind's centre,
Received, embraced my naked intuition.
The town of Nilburg too I shrank to enter

(If memory serves me right) and wept contrition
For indistinct all-but-committed crimes
In gelding-rooms and caves of parturition.

Yet undeniably I laughed at times
With those who shared my headless hullaballoo:
Fogeaters, Dwarfs, Green Quims and Paradigms.

Cellars of Nilburg! how I hated you,
Your Ixion wheels, hot frogs and icy toads,
Your existential climate where I grew

Into an adult mandrake. (Memory loads
My plate with mushrooms.) But I woke at length
And left you, travelling light by mountain roads
To Elsewhere; drank at desert wells; gained strength.

## Elephanta

Accordion and sweet brisk drum
Waken a lounging passion

Outside the wooden teashop where a young
Black-trousered androgynous dancer

Trounces the dust, crooking a maggot's finger,
While pockmarked queers applaud and smoke.

Great hawks like monoplanes
Above the bony tamarind,

Above the quarried rock sail high, high,
And Shiva like a business uncle watches

The village girls with cans to fill
File through the temple to a covered cistern.

Consider. Seasnake, white cloud minnow,
Octopus and moray eel,

Lovely in their lit aquariums
Breathe water as we do,

Have the advantage that they cannot feel.
Yet I have seen, across an angry tide-rip,

The narrow coffin-boat, the catamaran,
Go simply as a girl, with forward-leaning

Mast and torn triangular sail,
Leaving a crowded net behind.


## A Prospect of Old Age

Suppose a nest of bees, their honey staining
Brown brittle paper on the wall:
A sun dried hut of bricks, bone-dry
Kiln for the hermit years remaining.

Let this man work entirely to recapture
The aerial music of his youth,
Or talk with angels as the carnal
Agony subsides. A stony rapture

This would be. Revengeful, as if joking,
Cheat Caesar by apparent death,
Deny his relatives their pound of flesh,
To criticize his smell, his cough, his smoking.

Let that sweet corrosive dream
More dangerous than Simeon Stylites'
Take shape: an old man at his prayers,
Self-gutted, tugged from the human stream,

An old grey gander with no goose
Who wakes in moonlight groaning for
The dead to answer. Hears above his head
The cranky shutter clatter loose.

## Ballad of Calvary Street

On Calvary Street are trellises
Where bright as blood the roses bloom,
And gnomes like pagan fetishes
Hang their hats on an empty tomb
Where two old souls go slowly mad,
National Mum and Labour Dad.

Each Saturday when full of smiles
The children come to pay their due,
Mum takes down the family files
And cover to cover she thumbs them through,
Poor Len before he went away
And Mabel on her wedding day.

The meal-brown scones display her knack,
Her polished oven spits with rage,
While in Grunt Grotto at the back
Dad sits and reads the Sporting Page,
Then ambles out in boots of lead
To weed around the parsnip bed.

A giant parsnip sparks his eye,
Majestic as the Tree of Life;
He washes it and rubs it dry
And takes it in to his old wife –
'Look Laura, would that be a fit?
The bastard has a flange on it!'

When both were young she would have laughed,
A goddess in her tartan skirt,
But wisdom, age and mothercraft
Have rubbed it home that men like dirt:
Five children and a fallen womb,
A golden crown beyond the tomb.

Nearer the bone, sin is sin,
And women bear the cross of woe,
And that affair with Mrs Flynn
(It happened thirty years ago)
Though never mentioned, means that he
Will get no sugar in his tea.

The afternoon goes by, goes by,
The angels harp above a cloud;
A son-in-law with spotted tie

And daughter Alice fat and loud
Discuss the virtues of insurance
And stuff their tripes with trained endurance.

Flood-waters hurl upon the dyke
And Dad himself can go to town,
For little Charlie on his trike
Has ploughed another iris down.
His parents rise to chain the beast,
Brush off the last crumbs of their lovefeast.

And so these two old fools are left,
A rosy pair in evening light,
To question Heaven's dubious gift,
To hag and grumble, growl and fight:
The love they kill won't let them rest,
Two birds that peck in one fouled nest.

Why hammer nails? Why give no change?
Habit, habit clogs them dumb.
The Sacred Heart above the range
Will bleed and burn till Kingdom Come,
But Yin and Yang won't ever meet
In Calvary Street, in Calvary Street.


## Evidence at the Witch Trials

No woman's pleasure did I feel
    Under the hazel tree
When heavy as a sack of meal
    The Black Man mounted me,
But cold as water from a dyke
    His seed that quickened me.

What his age I cannot tell;
    Foul he was, and fair.
There blew between us both from Hell
    A blast of grit and fire,
And like a boulder is the babe
    That in my womb I bear.

Though I was youngest in that band
    Yet I was quick to learn.
A red dress he promised me

43

And red the torches burn.
Between the faggot and the flame
I see his face return.


## Winter

Winter unbundles a sack of storms
Above the flat scrub country.

Far at sea a trawling captain
Watches a double rainbow arching,
Noah's good sign, along the black horizon,
Hopes for groper, fat cod, terakihi.

A bureaucrat lights the gas fire
That warms his raw-edged afternoon,
Plucks a folder from a grey steel file,
Coughs, and eyes the telephone.

A housewife sees her washing, three-days-wet,
Hang draggled in the tugging wind,
Measures the old chair for new covers,
An ache of winter in the mind.

A child dawdling home from school
Builds little twig dams in the gutter,
Sings to himself although his shoes
Are damp, and bullies lurk at Butcher's Corner.

Winter unwraps a parcel of stones
For old and sick and sad, and homeless walkers.


## On the Death of her Body

It is a thought breaking the granite heart
Time has given me, that my one treasure,
Your limbs, those passion-vines, that bamboo body

Should age and slacken, rot
Some day in a ghastly clay-stopped hole.
They led me to the mountains beyond pleasure

Where each is not gross body or blank soul
But a strong harp the wind of genesis
Makes music in, such resonant music

44

That I was Adam, loosened by your kiss
From time's hard bond, and you,
My love, in the world's first summer stood

Plucking the flowers of the abyss.

## Election 1960

Hot sun. Lizards frolic
Fly-catching on the black ash

That was green rubbish. Tiny dragons,
They dodge among the burnt broom stems

As if the earth belonged to them
Without condition. In the polling booths

A democratic people have elected
King Log, King Stork, King Log, King Stork again.

Because I like a wide and silent pond
I voted Log. That party was defeated.

Now frogs will dive and scuttle to avoid
That poking idiot bill, the iron gullet:

Delinquent frogs! Stork is an active King,
A bird of principle, benevolent,

And Log is Log, an old time-serving post
Hacked from a totara when the land was young.

## Ballad of John Silent

To Babylon town
At morning I came
Looking for someone
To tell me my name,

From brown hills and wide water,
From my father's garden,
From my brother's joking,
From my mother's kitchen,

Ignorant and early
And not very big,
With my soul inside me
Like a ferret in a bag.

Men with money,
Men with books,
Followed me with monkeys
Riding on their backs,

Chattering, 'Listen, boy,
Make it a deal!
You can have the whole town
For your brand new soul.'

'Tell me my name then.'
'We don't know.'
They frowned and they threatened
But I went by,

Past the hospital gate
And the railway line,
Past the Grand Hotel
And the church so fine,

To a house where a woman
Was leaning on a door
With eyes like the sunset
And a flower in her hair.

'Lady, can you tell me
My own true name?'
'Yes, John Silent –
Come in, John.'

On a big brass bed
I laid her down.
Out of the bag
The ferret sprang,

Quicker than I say it
Out through the keyhole
Wriggled and vanished
My red-eyed soul.

'Do you love me, John?'
'Why, yes, I do.'
'Then sing me a song
While I play with you.'

'I can sing no song
When my soul is gone.'
'Then tell me a story,
Silent John.'

'To Babylon town
At daybreak I came
Looking for someone
To tell me my name,

'From sour hills and wild water,
From my father's truncheon,
From my brother's envy,
From my mother's bitching,

'And lucky I found
A woman for a blacksmith
To forge me the fetters
I go to my death with.'


### Brown Bone

*Bone in the river bed,*
*Old bone like a honeycomb,*
*Brown bone, man bone,*
*Where do you come from?*

I camped on a shingle flat
Beside the loud Rakaia,
And drove my tent pegs in
And built a fire of dry manuka.

I'd bread in the saddlebags
And tea in the black billy
And enough tobacco to last me
All the way to Gabriel's Gully.

I stretched out like a log
Dreaming of girls and cider,
And Death came like a riding man
With hooves of mountain water.

*Bone in the river bed,*
*Old bone cracked by the sun,*
*Brown bone like a honeycomb,*
*Don't take it hard, man.*

## Brighton

Glass-fronted baches stand and look
On the brown hurdling waves

That die at a brackish river mouth
Choked by the sand at every tide.

A township full of ears! They used to send
A springcart round the sandhills to bring in

The drunken elders. Toi-toi, marram grass,
Teach nothing to the narrow church of tin.

Beyond the high-banked green domain
Where boy and girl lying in lupin mazes

Pluck the dragon's apple, older now,
I go on beaches when the tide is low

And fish for poems where my four dead uncles,
Jack, Billy, Mark and Sandy,

Let down their lines from laps of broken stone
For the fat red cod and small-mouthed greenbone.

## At Taieri Mouth

Flax-pods unload their pollen
Above the steel-bright cauldron

Of Taieri, the old water-dragon
Sliding out from a stone gullet

Below the Maori-ground. Scrub horses
Come down at night to smash the fences

Of the whaler's children. Trypots have rusted
Leaving the oil of anger in the blood

Of those who live in two-roomed houses
Mending nets or watching from a window

The great south sky fill up with curdled snow.
Their cows eat kelp along the beaches.

The purple sailor drowned in thighboots
Drifting where the currents go

Cannot see the flame some girl has lighted
In a glass chimney, but in five days' time

With bladder-weed around his throat
Will ride the drunken breakers in.


## The Rubber Monkey

Very late at night my son's red monkey
Crouches on the bookshelf, ready
To beat a tom-tom automatically

If you squeeze the bulb. It is
A relevant emblem. Operation Phoebus
Equally rubs out stupidities

And honourable speeches. There will come
From radio dials a speechless hum,
The rubber monkey whacks his drum

And mushrooms grow above the cities
Cruelly dissolving in their furnace
The powers of youth and age, the flask of pities.


## The Ballad of Grady's Dream

One clink black night in June
Concrete Grady sat
Between the knees of the pines
With Old Jack Flynn his mate,

And through the harbour fog
The guts of Wellington
Glowed like a great morgue
Where even the cops had gone.

49

'I had a dream,' said Grady –
Flynn said, 'Stuff your dream!
I'd give my ballocks now
For a bucket of steam.'

'I had a dream,' said Grady,
When I slept in Mulligan's woodyard
Under a wad of roofing iron;
I was a white bird,

'And then a gale caught me
And threw me north;
There was nothing left standing
On the bare-arsed earth,

'And I thought of the time in Crete
When we jammed the Bren gun
And the paratroops came over
Like washing on a line,

'And you'll remember, Jack,
Because you were there,
We shot twelve prisoners
In Imvros village square;

'Because the wind blew me
To the door of a stone barn,
And the Nazi lads were sitting
At a table playing cards –

'*Sergeant, come in*, they said,
*We've kept you a place* –
And when they turned I saw
The red-hot bone in each one's face,

'So I let the wind carry
Me out past Kapiti
In the belly of the storm above
A thousand miles of sea,

'Till I came to a blind cliff
That got no sun,
Deep as the cunning of Hell
And high as the trouble of man.

'There was one gap in it
Where only a bird could fly;

I said the Hail Mary
And threaded the needle's eye,

'And there in a green garden
I saw the Tramways Band
And a crowd of people walking
With flagons in their hands,

'And on a bullock wagon
The Host Itself with seven nuns,
And one of them had the face
Of Rose O'Rourke when she was young.'

'You've struck it there,' said Flynn,
'She'd be a bit of all right;
But I'd give old Rose the go-by
For a bottle of steam tonight.

## The Tree

Nothing was evil then. The editing came later.
Thirty years back, down time's rock shaft, I see,
Too early for the heart-and-arrow sign,
A tree of vulvas oozing golden resin
Where I and my wire-muscled cousin
Climbed endlessly. Its bird-shit-spattered branches
Invoked the gross maternal mystery
That fed his life and mine.

Smoking my father's tobacco in a sly
Tree house, or edging up a shaking mast
To a cradle open to the sky,
Riding those giant fronded arms,
I seemed to be included by
The wind in its long conversation
About some secret known to birds or men;
Perhaps what made my uncle die;

Something too hard for words. My cousin,
Climbing the ladder after me,
Would call me barmy, slither down the tree
Like an opossum, wrestle with
Scissors and headlock, order me to try on
His boxing gloves. And fighting him
I quite forgot I carried in my pocket
Green macrocarpa nuts, the seeds of time.

## At Serrières

Blue water of the Rhône in its rock bed
Stalling, circling in pools behind
The island lousy with snakes: down I sank
With stones inside my bathing dress
To the mud bottom, to walk like a crab,

All that green summer drank
Air, knowledge. Bitter tough-skinned grapes
In a wild hilltop vineyard,
And the days, the days, like long loaves
Broken in half, as I fished with a cord

And a pierced stone for Yvette, the manager's daughter,
Killing hens in the hotel courtyard.
That castle where my brother broke his arm,
Yes: convolvulus vines, starved ghosts in dungeons . . .
But the family album does not include

The new guitar of sex I kept on twanging
Inside the iron virgin
Of the little smelly dyke, or that Easter Sunday,
Through a chink in the bedclothes, watching my mother
     dressing:
The heavy thighs, the black bush of hair.

Those wild red grapes were bitter
Though you could not tell them, by just looking, from the
     table kind.

## The Hollow Place

On the waste low headland
Below the road, above the plunging sea,
I would climb often round the crumbling face
Where flax bushes precariously
Gave something to grip: then I'd stand
Alive in the hollow place
That meant . . . well, I must describe it: a bent cleft
In limestone rock above a pool
Of fluttering scum; bushes to the left,
And an overhang. The passage was dark and cool,
Three yards long perhaps, hidden from any eye
Not acquainted; and the air
Tainted by some odour as if the earth sweated

In primeval sleep. I did nothing there;
There was nothing to do but listen to some greater I
Whose language was silence. Again and again I came
And was healed of the daftness, the demon in the head
And the black knot in the thighs, by a silence that
Accepted all. Not knowing I would come again,
My coat of words worn very thin,
Knocking, as if lame,
With a dry stick on the dumb
Door of the ground, and crying out:
'Open, mother. Open. Let me in.'


## The Cold Hub

Lying awake on a bench in the town belt,
Alone, eighteen, more or less alive,
Lying awake to the sound of clocks,
The railway clock, the Town Hall clock,
And the Varsity clock, genteel, exact
As a Presbyterian conscience,
I heard the hedgehogs chugging round my bench,
Colder than an ice-axe, colder than a bone,
Sweating the booze out, a spiritual Houdini
Inside the padlocked box of winter, time and craving.

Sometimes I rolled my coat and put it under my head,
And when my back got frozen, I put it on again.
I thought of my father and mother snoring at home
While the fire burnt out in feathery embers.
I thought of my friends each in their own house
Lying under blankets, tidy as dogs or mice.
I thought of my med. student girlfriend
Dreaming of horses, cantering brown-eyed horses,
In her unreachable bed, wrapped in a yellow quilt,

And something bust inside me, like a winter clod
Cracked open by the frost. A sense of being at
The absolute unmoving hub
From which, to which, the intricate roads went.
Like Hemingway, I call it *nada:*
*Nada*, the Spanish word for nothing.
*Nada;* the belly of the whale; *nada;*
*Nada;* the little hub of the great wheel;
*Nada;* the house on Cold Mountain
Where the east and the west wall bang together;
*Nada;* the drink inside the empty bottle.

53

You can't get there unless you are there.
The hole in my pants where the money falls out,
That's the beginning of knowledge; *nada*.

It didn't last for long; it never left me.
I knew that I was *nada*. Almost happy,
Stiff as a giraffe, I called in later
At an early grill, had coffee, chatted with the boss.

That night, drunk again, I slept much better
At the bus station, in a broom cupboard.


## The Last Judgement

The children have more sense than to be sad
Tucked down – my daughter loiters and my son
Grizzles about a picture he'd begun
And screwed and burnt. Hugging can knock the bad
Mood back; long hugging. I'm left alone to look

At Breughel's *Judgement* in a book
Which proves by symbols the Unconscious Mind
Makes Hell and Heaven. Are you blind,
Old man? the smoke of Tartarus
Was never hard to find;

   *Quando judex est venturus . . .*
My friend at half-past five in a lounge bar
Told me he thought the world had hair around it
Like Breughel's whale's-mouth Pit
Down which an army plunges. He'd just bought

The latest make of English car
With automatic gears for his third wife
To ride in, ride, self-taught,
Past the skull signs, to endless life,
To Mary Baker Eddy's world of thought

Or the stony gully of Jehoshaphat
Where the dead rise. I know that boneless mouth,
The owl, the dragon and the fish;
Long hugging cannot make it nice
To be laid out alive upon a dish

Under the eye and claw of the clever cat . . .
But there is pity, pity, wind of the South

54

That blows to some rose garden where
My dead grandmother in her old cane chair
Smiles at the Judge and strokes the quivering mice.


## On Reading Yevtushenko

When the mine exploded at Kaitangata
Trucks flew out as if from the barrel of a gun,
Trucks and truckers, bodies of men,
Or so my father told me;
                              and far down
In those dark passages they heard faintly
The waves of the sea hammer
Above their heads.
                        My father's hands are corded
With swollen veins, but my hands are thinner
And my thoughts are cold, Zhenya Yevtushenko;
They are covered with black dust.
                                      Reading you
I remember our own strangled Revolution:
1935. The body of our Adam was dismembered
By statisticians.
                      I would like to meet you
Quietly in a café, where hoboes and freckled girls
Drink, talk; not to pump you; only to revalue in your company
Explosions, waves of the sea.


## Waipatiki Beach

### 1

Under rough kingly walls the black-and-white
Sandpiper treads on stilts the edges

Of the lagoon, whose cry is like
A creaking door. We came across the ridges

By a bad road, banging in second gear,
Into the only world I love:

This wilderness. Through the noon light rambling clear
Foals and heifers in the green paddocks move.

The sun is a shepherd. Once I would have wanted
The touch of flesh to cap and seal my joy,

Not yet having sorted it out. Bare earth, bare sea,
Without fingers crack open the hard ribs of the dead.


## 2

If anyone, I'd say the oldest Venus
Too early for the books, ubiquitous,

The manifold mother to whom my poems go
Like ladders down – at the mouth of the gully

She had left a lip of sand for the coarse grass to grow,
Also the very quiet native bee

Loading his pollen bags. We parked the car
There, and walked on

Down to the bank of the creek, where the water ran under
A froth of floating sticks and pumice stone,

And saw in the dune's clasp the burnt black
Trunk of a totara the sea had rolled back.


## 3

Her lion face, the skull-brown Hekate
Ruling my blood since I was born,

I had not found it yet. I and my son
Went past the hundred-headed cabbage tree

At the end of the beach, barefooted, in danger of
Stones falling from the overhang, and came

On a bay too small to have a name
Where flax grew wild on the shoulder of the bluff

And a waterfall was weeping. A sheep leapt and stood
Bleating at us beyond a tangle of driftwood

And broken planks. Behind us floated in the broad noon
Sky that female ghost, the daylight moon.

*4*

A leper's anger in the moon's disc, or
The long-tongued breaker choked by sand,

Spell out my years like Pharaoh's wheat and husk –
I walk and look for shelter from the wind

Where many feet have trodden
Till silence rises and the beach is hidden.

### An Ode to the Reigning Monarch on the Occasion of Her Majesty's Visit to Pig Island

Madam, I beg to quarrel with
Your trip across the water –
Pig Island needs no English myth
To keep its guts in order,
Though our half-witted housewives yearn
At your image on the TV screen.

Forgive me that I cannot praise
The Civil Service State
Whose blueprints falsify the maze
It labours to create,
And plants above that sticky mess
Yourself in an icing sugar dress.

The dead who drink at Bellamys
Are glad when school kids clap
A Fairy Queen who justifies
The nabob and the bureaucrat,
In a land where a wharfie's daughter can
Marry some day the squatter's son.

While the stuffed monkey, dog and sow,
Play ludo in the void,
The Auckland pavements carry now
Six hundred unemployed,
And the bought clerks who sneer at them
Will crowd to kiss your diadem.

The girls in Arohata jail
Are very rarely dressed in silk –
Let us take a Glasgow cocktail
Bubbling coal gas into milk,
Drink up to Mary, Kate and Lou,
No better and no worse than you.

Before my birth your soldiers made
A football of my skull
At Mud Farm when they crucified
My father on a pole
Because he would not take a gun
And kill another working man.

I give you now to end our talk
A toast you will not like:
MacSweeney the Lord Mayor of Cork
Who died on hunger strike.
It took him eighty days to drown
In the blood and shit that floats the Crown.

While Big Ben bangs out stroke on stroke
And the circus wheel spins round,
The Maori looks at Holyoake
And Holyoake looks at the ground,
And there will be more things to say
When the Royal yacht has sailed away.


## Dragon's Hour

Pillars of fire!
It is the lost temple
in which that raging void, Adam's desire
to be a god, grows ample

and overshadows us. The calm sea
quakes; the imponderable
tears of apocalypse on field and city
fall,

on children's limbs, on veins of the breast,
quenching the daystar
with blood; as in their youths our fathers dreamt they saw
the fire-drake rising from his cloudy nest.

58

## Shingle Beach Poem

There is (conveniently) a hollow space
Between the upper and the lower jaws

Of the world serpent. There, as if all days
Were one, the children whack

Their seaweed balls, brag, tussle, comb the shores
For little crabs. There's no road back

To the dream time, and I endure instead
This hunger to be nothing. I supplicate

Dark heaven for the peace of that woman they
Lifted out of the breakers yesterday,

With blue deaf ears, whom Poseidon banged on the kelp-beds
Though she was a good swimmer, her body oatmeal-white

Spotted with shingle. To and fro
She was rolled by the undertow.

This I understand. Sister, remember
Us who wrestle yet in the coil of life's hunger.

## Morning Train

Those heavy clouds drifting above
The harbour basin, warehouse, railway yard,

At 7 a.m. may remind the guard
Who punches my ticket that he has forgotten to shave,

Or look like the breasts of his wife. To me they look
Like the rafters of Hades. My fellow-travellers have

Faces of tired rock. I watch them go
Like mountains walking, through the den of shadows

To forges and wheels. They do not need a book
To tell them where they are, in the burrows of the grave,

Indifferent to any truth revealed,
Wearing the brass helmet of monotony,

Whose fathers saw grief as a hailstorm in the fields
Or branches torn away from a rotten tree.

## East Coast Journey

About twilight we came to the whitewashed pub
On a knuckle of land above the bay

Where a log was riding and the slow
Bird-winged breakers cast up spray.

One of the drinkers round packing cases had
The worn face of a kumara god,

Or so it struck me. Later on
Lying awake in the veranda bedroom

In great dryness of mind I heard the voice of the sea
Reverberating, and thought: As a man

Grows older he does not want beer, bread, or the prancing fles
But the arms of the eater of life, Hine-nui-te-po,

With teeth of obsidian and hair like kelp
Flashing and glimmering at the edge of the horizon.

## Pig Island Letters

### (to Maurice Shadbolt)

#### 1

The gap you speak of – yes, I find it so,
The menopause of the mind. I think of it
As a little death, practising for the greater,
For the undertaker who won't have read
Your stories or my verse –
Or that a self had died
Who handled ideas like bombs,

In that bare southern town
At a party on a cold night
Men seen as ghosts, women like trees walking,
Seen from the floor, a forest of legs and bums
For the climbing boy, the book-bred one.

And this, the moment of art, can never stay.
Wives in the kitchen cease to smile as we go
Into the gap itself, the solid night
Where poor drunks fear the icy firmament:
Man is a walking grave,

That is where I start from. Though often
Where the Leith Stream wandered down
Its culvert, crinkled labia of blossom
On the trees beside the weir
Captured and held the fugitive
From time, from self, from the iron pyramid,

These were diversions. Give my love
To Vic. He is aware of
The albatross. In the Otago storms
Carrying spray to salt the landward farms
The wind is a drunkard. Whoever can listen
Long enough will write again.


2


From an old house shaded with macrocarpas
Rises my malady.
Love is not valued much in Pig Island
Though we admire its walking parody,

That brisk gaunt woman in the kitchen
Feeding the coal range, sullen
To all strangers, lest one should be
Her antique horn-red Satan.

Her man, much battled, grousing in the pub,
Discusses sales
Of yearling lambs, the timber in a tree
Thrown down by autumn gales,

Her daughter, reading in her room
A catalogue of dresses,
Can drive a tractor, goes to Training College,
Will vote on the side of the Bosses,

Her son is moodier, has seen
An angel with a sword
Standing above the clump of old man manuka
Just waiting for the word

To overturn the cities and the rivers
And split the house like a rotten totara log.
Quite unconcerned he sets his traps for 'possums
And whistles to his dog.

The man who talks to the masters of Pig Island
About the love they dread
Plaits ropes of sand, yet I was born among them
And will lie some day with their dead.

### 3

That other Baxter the Sectarian
Said that the bodies of the damned will burn
Like stubble thrown into a red-hot oven
On Judgement Day. In Calvin's town
At seventeen I thought I might see
Not fire but water rise

From the shelves of surf beyond St Clair
To clang the dry bell. Gripping
A pillow wife in bed
I did my convict drill,
And when I made a mother of the keg
The town split open like an owl's egg
Breaking the ladders down. It was
Perhaps the winter of beginning:

Frost standing up like stubble in the streets
Below the knees of Maori Hill,
Looking for the last simplicity
And nothing to explain it in the books,
In a room where the wind clattered the blind-cord
In the bed of a girl with long plaits
I found the point of entry,
The place where father Adam died.

Meanwhile a boy with dog and ferret
Climbed up the gorse track from the sea
To the turn at the top of the gully
Twelve paces past the cabbage tree,
And saw from the crest of the hill
Pillars of rain move on the dark sea,
A cloud of fire rise up above Japan,
God's body blazing on damnation's tree.

Thank you for the letter. I read your book
Five days ago: it has the slow
Imperceptible wingbeat of the hawk
Above the dry scrublands. The kill is there
In the Maori riverbed below
Where bones glitter. I could tell
Of other matters, but not now.


4

The censor will not let my lines reveal
Pig Island spinning on the potter's wheel.

A skinny wench in jeans with a kea's eye:
The rack on which our modern martyrs die.

I prophesy these young delinquent bags
Will graduate to grim demanding hags.

Our women chiefly carry in their bones
The curse that stuck to the scattered oven stones.

How often Remuera girls abort
Has not been mentioned in the Hunn Report.

Holyoake yammering from a kauri stump –
God save us all! I need a stomach pump.

Sea-eggs, puha, pork, and kumara:
The Maori owned the land. I have a camera.

Though Freud and God may bless the marriage vow
You must know how to work the hillside plough.

The sun is warm, the nosebag smells of hay,
The wind is blowing from the north today.

You who were pulled apart by four draught horses,
Saint Hippolytus, pray for us!


5

Long ago, in a ghostly summer,
Somebody held a burning-glass
Above the ants on mountains of crumbed asphalt,

63

So that one lived, another died:
The hawk's eye, the man in the sky
With his vats of poison cloud
Like Jeyes Fluid. Above the old river
The bridge was a broad mother,
And the small drum of the heart beat loud,

Where the salt gush flowed in
Hooking the fish of Maui on a pin.

To learn the tricks of water
From the boathouse keeper's daughter
Is the task of time. I make
My genuflection at an iron altar
Before the black fish rise, the weather break.


6

The hope of the body was coherent love
As if the water sighing on the shores
Would penetrate the hardening muscle, loosen
Whatever had condemned itself in us:
Not the brown flagon, not the lips
Anonymously pressed in the dim light,
But a belief in bodily truth rising
From fountains of Bohemia and the night,

The truth behind the lie behind the truth
That Fairburn told us, gaunt
As the great moa, throwing the twisted blunt
Darts in a pub this side of Puhoi – 'No
Words make up for what we had in youth.'
For what we did not have: that hunger caught
Each of us, and left us burnt,
Split open, grit-dry, sifting the ash of thought.


7

This love that heals like a crooked limb
In each of us, source of our grief,
Could tell us if we cared to listen, why
Sons by mayhem, daughters by harlotry
Pluck down the sky's rage on settled houses:
The thin girl and the cornerboy
Whose angers mask their love

Unwind, unwind the bandages
That hide in each the hope of joy.

For me it is the weirs that mention
The love that we destroy
By long evasion, politics and art,
And speech that is a kind of contraception:
A streetlight flashing down
On muscled water, bodies in the shade,
Tears on a moonwhite face, the voice
Of time from the grave of water speaking to
Those who are lucky to be sad.


### 8

When I was only semen in a gland
Or less than that, my father hung
From a torture post at Mud Farm
Because he would not kill. The guards
Fried sausages, and as the snow came darkly
I feared a death by cold in the cold groin
And plotted revolution. His black and swollen thumbs
Explained the brotherhood of man,

But he is old now in his apple garden
And we have seen our strong Antaeus die
In the glass castle of the bureaucracies
Robbing our bread of salt. Shall Marx and Christ
Share beds this side of Jordan? I set now
Unwillingly these words down:

*Political action in its source is pure,*
*Human, direct, but in its civil function*
*Becomes the jail it laboured to destroy.*


### 9

Look at the simple caption of success,
The poet as family man,
Head between thumbs at mass, nailing a trolley,
Letting the tomcat in:
Then turn the hourglass over, find the other
Convict self, incorrigible, scarred
With what the bottle and the sex games taught,
The black triangle, the whips of sin.

The first gets all his meat from the skull-faced twin,
Sharpening a dagger out of a spoon,
Struggling to speak through the gags of a poem:
When both can make a third my work is done.

Nor will the obituary ever indicate
How much we needed friends,
Like Fitz at the National
Speaking of his hydatid cyst,
A football underneath the lung,
Or Lowry in Auckland: all who held the door
And gave us space for art,
Time for the re-shaping of the heart:
Those whom the arrow-makers honour least,
Companions to the manbeast,
One man in many, touching the flayed hide gently,
A brother to the artist and a nurse.

The trees rustle as October comes
And fantails batter on the glass,
Season when the day nurse tuts and hums
Laying out pills and orange juice
For one who walks the bridge of dread
As oedema sets in,
While through the bogs and gullies of Pig Island
Bellies are beaten like skin drums
In pup tents, under flax or lupin shade,

As if the sun were a keg. And this man
On the postman's round will meditate
The horn of Jacob withered at the root
Or quirks of weather. None
Grow old easily. The poem is
A plank laid over the lion's den.


*10*


To outflank age – a corrugated shack
With fried pauas in the pan,
Beside a bay somewhere, grandchildren in tribes
Wrestling in the long grass, seawater, sleep,
While cloud and green tree like sisters keep
The last door for the natural man.

It will be what it is, half-life,
For the mystery requires
A victim – Marsyas the manbeast
Hung up and flayed on a fir tree,
Or a death by inches, catheter and wife
Troubling an old man's vanity.


## 11

Tonight I read my son a story
About the bees of Baiame, who tell the east wind
To blow down rain, so that the flowers grow
In dry Australia, and the crow *wirinun*
Who jailed the west wind in a hollow log:

My son who is able to build a tree house
With vine ladders, my son
In his brown knitted jersey and dungarees,
Makes clowns and animals, a world of creatures
To populate paradise,

And when he hands me easily
The key of entry, my joy must be dissembled
Under a shutter of horn, a dark lantern,
In case it should too brightly burn,

Because the journey has begun
Into the land where the sun is silent
And no one may enter the tree house
That hides the bones of a child in the forest of a man.


## 12

The dark wood Dante wrote of
Is no more than the self, the wandering gulf
That calls itself a man, seen
Through the dark prism of self-love:
Under the leafy screen
Lion, leopard, wolf,
Show by their anger we are not yet slain.

Our loves have tied us to the wheel
From which it is death to be unbound,
Yet unexpected, unpredictable,
Like speckled rain that falls on a wave,

67

Come the light fingers on the wound,
Or where the marae meets the cattle hill
The face of Beatrice moving in the grove.


## 13

*Stat crux dum volvitur orbis:* I will sing
In the whale's belly.
                              'Great Mother of God
Sweeten my foul breath. I wait for a death.
Cradle me, Lady, on the day they carry
My body down the bush track to the road
To the rollers of the decorous van.
The leper's stump, the thick voice of the drunk,
Are knocking at Nazareth. I am a naked man.'

'How can I let you in?
The time for talk has gone;
A mountain is the threshold stone.'

'Mother, I come alone.
No books, no bread
Are left in my swag.'

'Why are your hands not clean?'

'There was no soap in the whole damned town.'

'God's grace has need of man's apology.'

'Your face is my theology.'

'Yes; but I gave you a jewel to bring.'

'In the thick gorse of the gully
I lost your signet ring.'

'Why should I listen then?'

'On Skull Hill there was none,
No scapular, no sign,
Only the words, *I thirst*,
When the blood of a convict burst
From the body of your son.'

'You may come in.'

Is it like that? At least I know no better;
After a night of argument
Mythical, theological, political,
Somebody has the sense to get a boat
And row out towards the crayfish rocks
Where, diving deep, the downward swimmer
Finds fresh water rising up,
A mounded water breast, a fountain,
An invisible tree whose roots cannot be found;

As that wild nymph of water rises
So does the God in man.

## Letter to Robert Burns

King Robert, on your anvil stone
Above the lumbering Octagon,
To you I raise a brother's horn
Led by the wandering unicorn
Of total insecurity.
Never let your dead eye look
Up from Highland Mary's book
To the fat scrag-end of the Varsity.
Kilmarnock hag and dominie
Watch there the grey Leith water drum
With laughter from a bird's beak
At what their learning has left out.
They tried to make my devil speak
With the iron boot of education
(Psychology, French, Latin) –
But though they drove the wedges in
Till the blood and marrow spouted out,
That spirit was dumb.

Robert, only a heart I bring,
No gold of words to grace a king,
Nor can a stranger lift that flail
That cracked the wall of Calvin's jail
And earned you the lead garland of
A people's moralizing love,
Till any Scotsman with the shakes
Can pile on your head his mistakes
And petrify a boozaroo
Reciting *Tam o' Shanter* through;
And there's an old black frost that freezes
Apollo's balls and the blood of Jesus

69

In this dry, narrow-gutted town.
Often enough I stumbled down
From Maori Hill to the railway station
(When Aussie gin was half the price)
Making my Easter meditation
In the wilderness of fire and ice
Where a Puritan gets his orientation.

King Robert with the horn of stone!
Perhaps your handcuffs were my own;
Your coffin-cradle was the blank
Medusa conscience of a drunk
That hankers for the purity
Of an imagined infancy,
And after riding seven whores
Approaches God upon all fours,
Crying, 'O thou great Incubus,
Help me or turn me to a walrus!'
And in hangover weeps to see
A playing child or a walnut tree.
If, lying in the pub latrine,
You muttered, 'Take me back to Jean,'
The reason for your mandrake groans
Is wrapped like wire around my bones.

Not too far from the Leith water
My mother saw the mandrake grow
And pulled it. A professor's daughter,
She told me some time after how
She had been frightened by a cow
So that the birth-sac broke too soon
And on the twenty-ninth of June
Prematurely I looked at the walls
And yelled. The Plunket nurse ran in
To scissor off my valued foreskin,
But one thing staggered that grimalkin:
Poets are born with three balls.

Biology, mythology,
Go underground when the bookmen preach,
And I must thank the lass who taught me
My catechism at Tunnel Beach;
For when the hogmagandie ended
And I lay thunder-struck and winded,
The snake-haired Muse came out of the sky
And showed her double axe to me.
Since then I die and do not die.

'Jimmy,' she said, 'you are my ugliest son;
I'll break you like a herring-bone.'

I fill my pipe with black tobacco
And watch a dead man's ember glow.


## The First Communions

### (after Rimbaud)

### 1

It makes me want to laugh, those country churches
Where fifteen kids like ugly ducklings
Dirty the pillars, quack, talk back
To an old daft priest in greasy shoes:
Being instructed!
                And the sun glitters through leaves;
Light roosts in the windows like broken loaves.

The stone smells always of the earth it came from;
Boulders just like these are piled
Where the earth trembles on heat.
                        Rose-bushes, briars
Climb over them, and the heavy-headed wheat
Pushes up through the crevices
In the belly of the ground, the earth's old dried scars.

Once in a hundred years they wash these churches,
Like barns, with curds of milk and blue water.
Flies out of the pub and the cowshed gather
To eat the wax of candle-droppings
Down there, below the peeled paint
Of Madonna and Saint.

But the kids must think of their Dads and Mums
Each doing a lifetime of hard labour:
Good peasant stock!
                  They scat, with red necks crawling where
Christ's Priest has touched them: Old Iron Fingers. He goes glum
To a house shaded by sycamores
And well paid for. The kids are alive in the sun

For a day at least.
                O first black suits! Jam tarts!
Plates on doilies under Napoleon's picture
For the Josephs and the Marthas who'll meet at the rail

With tongues stuck out, two halves of a map
That's not yet one.
                        The First Communion's flow of sap
Will come and go, and these things remain.

The girls who sit prim on the church benches are glad
When the boys whisper, 'Little bitches!'
Like monkeys in new jackets after Mass
Or sung Vespers, the brats crowd out
Snapping their fingers and jumping, singing bad ditties
At those shop-window dummies, the families in cafés.

In the meantime the fat old Priest picks out
A holy picture for each child.
He walks in his garden when the air is mild
And hears the fiddle-twang downstreet
Of distant dancing. He sketches a step; in his old bull's breast
    the night
Plunders like a bandit the gold towers of light.


2


One pupil he has noticed among the catechized
(Mostly children of the nobs) –
A strange little girl with sad eyes
And a white forehead. Her Dad has a caretaker's job.
'On that dear head, a Rachel among the catechized,
God will pour down His grace like a waterfall.'


3


The child's not well. She fidgets. Not yet inside the grim
Church, that cave of echoes, she is visited by
A shuddering fit. On the bed in her small high
Attic room she dreams of the conquering Victim.

'I am dying,' she whispers; crosses her hands and waits,
The smart one, stealing a march on the other girls.
Angels, Jesuses, Virgins whiter than pearl
Float through the ceiling. Her soul has opened its gates.

*Adonai!* . . . He rides on the rolling crest
Of Latin words. Green lightnings jump from the ice-browed
Sky. The stars are wrapped in a scrubbed white shroud
Mottled with blood from a virgin martyr's breast.

72

A child's vow of virginity made in a dream!
She bites on the freezing wafer of Ransom,
Purer than moats of lilies, fresher than ice-cream,
O Queen of Angels, your ice-crystals of pardon!


4

But the Virgin goes back into the book;
Often enough a prayer can snap like a stalk . . .
All she has left is an old missal's vellum,
A vile wood-cut, and the bronze-clad giant of Boredom.

And a vague wish like a wind begins to flurry
The chaste blue dream (rough as the hair of a goat
Saint Joseph's beard) – it tugs at the seamless coat
With which Christ hides a nude and human body.

She is yearning, yearning towards the core of the furnace,
Gripping the pillow tight to smother her cries,
Struggling in the net of a self-made paradise,
Mouth wet . . . The yards are loaded with faggots of darkness.

The kid reaches the end of her tether. With one
Hand, arching her body, she opens the blue
Bed-curtain, to let the fresh air through
On belly and breast that bake in the holy oven . . .


5

Later – waking at midnight – the window is gleaming
White; in the curtain's fold the moon drowns deep;
The whiteness of Sunday beckons her soul from sleep
To walk. She has had red dreams; and her nose is bleeding.

Hollow and pure, she raises the vase of her heart
To God, and thirsts for the taste of the dark fountain
That flows all night from a cleft in Moses' mountain
And heals the wounded earth. She hides in the skirt

Of the first Mother, unseeable Night, who gathers
All young hurt things into her cloudy arms;
She thirsts for the Night, whose waters of grey calm
Cannot be stained by the blood of human fever.

Victim and little wife – her star watches her walk
With a candle in her hand down to the courtyard
Where a jacket is hanging on a line above the hard
Stones . . . Her small ghost hears the ghosts of the roofs talk.


6

Her God's-night was spent in a shithouse under the sky.
Through holes in the roof the white air crowded in
To the fluttering candle, and a wild vine
Tumbled over a broken wall nearby;

And later yet, when low skies plated the bones
Of the houses with gold, and the steam of washing water
Dusted the shadows with a stink like sulphur,
A living heart of light glowed on the stones . . .


7

Who will speak the epitaph of pity,
Eaters of dung, warpers of all things made,
You hypocrites? – Will you spit at the walking dead
When her leper's clapper sounds in the tomb of the city?


8

When she has swallowed down the green sour fruit,
One sword-grey dawn, sad in the yoke of love,
She will see her man still hunched up, dreaming of
A million sky-born Marys, and cry out:

'Do you know I have killed you? I have taken
Mouth, heart, whatever a man is,
And I am rotting. Oh, to lie down loveless
In the waters of night, with the Dead, and never waken!

'I was young once, and Christ made me foul.
He crammed my throat with what I spew up now.
You've kissed my Gideon's Fleece; you've nuzzled my brow;
And I let it happen . . . A good time had by all!

'Men! You men! You don't know how it is:
How every woman is torn in half between
The conscience and the flesh. We roast in pain,
God's whores, each one of us, burnt black by kisses.

74

'At my first Communion I married the Cross.
Your touch, your words of love, are a shut book.
Think. My soul, and the flesh that you took,
Are boiling with the maggot-white kisses of Jesus!'


9


And the soul that rots and the soul that lacks light
Will feel Your hatred grip them like a nurse,
Having lain down on the bed of Your granite Curse,
From mountains of Eden rolling towards the night.

O Christ, Christ, You have taken our strength from us!
You pale God, nailing to Your altar bone
Since Golgotha the women You turn to stone,
Chained to the earth in grief, mounted by the incubus!


## Seven Year Old Poet

### (after Rimbaud)

The mother, shutting the schoolbook, walked off blind
And well content, not seeing the hatred of work behind
The child's bumpy forehead, and under the blue eyes
An enemy self not built to fraternize.

Obedient he'd drudge all day; a quite
Intelligent boy; but somehow the sour bite
Of hypocrisy showed in his habits. Passing along
Mildewed passages, he'd stick out his tongue
And clench both fists in his groin, watching the spark
Of tiny specks that floated in the dark
Under his eyelids.
                          If a door on the evening air
Was open, you'd see him gasp, half up the stair,
Like a drying frog, under the gulf of day
That hung from the roofs. He'd hide himself away
In summer, clubbed flat, torpid, in the dell
Of a latrine, peacefully drinking the smell,
And it was cool there.
                          Sometimes when winter moonlight
Had washed the bushes, and antiseptic night
Drove out the daytime odours, he'd lie at the foot
Of a wall behind the house, like a cabbage root
Half underground, rubbing his eyes in order

To see visions, and hear each scabbed leaf shudder.
Quite tragic! His companions were those bent
Children whose clothes have a smell of excrement,
Old-fashioned, black-earth-knuckled, sometimes toothless,
Talking together in idiot gentleness.

And if, catching him out in some foul act
Of pity, his worrying Mother grubbed round the fact
For evidence, out of sick love he'd raise
A screen, and she'd believe it – that blue-eyed liar's gaze!

The seven-year-old would make up yarns inside
His own head, of the wastes where Freedom glows like a bride:
Savannahs, great trees, suns and shores – He'd rush
To coloured magazines, and stare and blush
At Spanish and Italian girls.
                                    From time to time a wild
Tomboy, the next-door family's dragged-up child
Brown-eyed and skittish, would jump on his back from behind –
Just eight years old – tossing her plaits; and blind
As a weasel in a burrow, he'd use his teeth
To bite her bare arse from underneath
(She never wore pants) – then, bruised by her heels and her claws
He'd mooch to his room with the taste of her flesh in his jaws

Sundays in winter, hair flattened with brilliantine,
At the pedestal table, reading a salad-green-
Edged-Bible – he hated it. In the alcove at night
Millstone dreams would grind him, till day's light
Drying the sweats of terror, pink as a dove,
Came back to the gable.
                              God he did not love,
But men, men he saw at sunset, dark
From the sun's glare, strolling in smocks to the park
Where the town criers would make the crowd come
To grizzle or laugh at their words, by the thrice-heard roll
        of a drum.
– He dreamt of the grassy field, where light in waves
Rose up, with a smell like bread, from the groined caves
Waist-high, a place for love!
                                    And more than all else
He liked what is dark: as when, shut from the bells
In the barn of his room – not minding the icy damp
Of the blue walls, he would read of a rebel camp
Among drowned forests, leaden skies, great flowers

Of flesh in starry woods, Andean towers,
Giddiness, flight – while the street chattered below –
Face down, his blue eyes flickering to and fro,
He would live the novel – alone, stretched out on the pale
Coarse linen that caught the wind, a ship in full sail!

### Tomcat

This tomcat cuts across the
zones of the respectable
through fences, walls, following
other routes, his own. I see
the sad whiskered skull-mouth fall
wide, complainingly, asking

to be picked up and fed, when
I thump up the steps through bush
at 4 p.m. He has no
dignity, thank God! has grown
older, scruffier, the ash-
black coat sporting one or two

flowers like round stars, badges
of bouts and fights. The snake head
is seamed on top with rough scars:
old Samurai! He lodges
in cellars, and the tight furred
scrotum drives him into wars

as if mad, yet tumbling on
the rug looks female, Turkish-
trousered. His bagpipe shriek at
sluggish dawn dragged me out in
pyjamas to comb the bush
(he being under the vet

for septic bites): the old fool
stood, body hard as a board,
heart thudding, hair on end, at
the house corner, terrible,
yelling at something. They said,
'Get him doctored.' I think not.

## At Days Bay

To lie on a beach after
looking at old poems: how
slow untroubled by any
grouch of mine or yours, Father
Ocean tumbles in the bay
alike with solitary

divers, cripples, yelling girls
and pipestem kids. He does what
suits us all; and somewhere – there,
out there, where the high tight sails
are going – he wears a white
death flag of foam for us, far

out, for when we want it. So
on Gea's breast, the broad nurse
who bears with me, I think of
adolescence: that sad boy
I was, thoughts crusted with ice
on the treadmill of self-love,

Narcissus damned, who yet brought
like a coal in a hollow
stalk, the seed of fire that runs
through my veins now. I praise that
sad boy now, who having no
hope, did not blow out his brains.


## Postman

To set a bound to chaos
(put it that way) the streets are
named, the houses numbered – but
foot-slogging over wet grass
or asphalt, the postman's dour
thought will sprout new chaos, not

original – so I find
as the housewives' donkey, bare-
shirted in the rain. The small
dogs muttering from the ground
smell me out, as I stagger,
and nip at the lifted heel

from paranoid love. I plod
up Motueka, Colway,
Karamu, each cold street a
dragon, and I stuck inside
the arse-pipe, a mildewed, slowly moving turd. These roads were

built for the helicopter
or bullock-dray. The boxes
(made roomy, narrow, or with
iron flaps) exhibit your
private shapes, you grim ladies
married to a bourgeois death

who wait for letters from God,
and as my hand goes in, I
think kindly of you all – 'Yes,
Mrs Cokestacker, your strayed
parcel from Melbourne may be
in the bag' – or, the Abyss . . .


## To a Print of Queen Victoria

I advise rest; the farmhouse
we dug you up in has been
modernized, and the people
who hung you as their ikon
against the long passage wall
are underground – Incubus

and excellent woman, we
inherit the bone acre
of your cages and laws. This
dull green land suckled at your
blood's *frigor Anglicanus*,
crowning with a housewife's tally

the void of Empire, does not
remember you – and certain
bloody bandaged ghosts rising
from holes of Armageddon
at Gallipoli or Sling
Camp, would like to fire a shot

through the gilt frame. I advise
rest, Madam; and yet the tomb

holds much that we must travel
barely without. Your print – 'from
an original pencil
drawing by the Marchioness

'of Granby, March, eighteen ninety seven . . .' Little mouth, strong
nose and hooded eye – they speak
of half-truths my type have slung
out of the window, and lack
and feel the lack too late. Queen,

you stand most for the time of
early light, clay roads, great trees
unfelled, and the smoke from huts
where girls in sack dresses
stole butter . . . The small rain spits
today. You smile in your grave.


## A Bucket of Blood for a Dollar

*(a conversation between Uncle Sam
and the Rt. Hon. Keith Holyoake,
Prime Minister of New Zealand)*

'You'll have to learn,' said Uncle Sam,
'The Yankee way of work
Now that you've joined in our crusade
Against the modern Turk;
The capital of the Commonwealth is
Not London, but New York.'

'Don't tell them that,' cried Holyoake,
'In Thames or Dannevirke.'

'Then use your loaf,' said Uncle Sam,
'Newspapers hit the eye;
If you get trouble from the men
That you can't bluff or buy,
Just spread the word that they're all Reds
And let the rumours fly.'

'I'll bang the drum,' said Holyoake –
And yet he heaved a sigh.

80

'Tell them straight,' said Uncle Sam,
'That it's a dirty war;
Mention the Freedom of the West
That we are fighting for;
But keep the money side of it
Well tucked behind the door.'

'I'll make it sound,' said Holyoake,
'Just like a football score.'

'Between the fights,' said Uncle Sam,
'They'll need some exercise;
There's a thousand brothels in Saigon
Where they can fraternize.
The peasants send their daughters there
When they have no rice.'

'Let's not be coarse,' said Holyoake,
Turning up his eyes.

'I fried a village,' said Uncle Sam,
'With the new phosphorus bomb
The day a Yankee Army nurse
Was killed by the Viet Cong;
A white dame's worth a million gooks –
In Asia, *we* belong.'

'Your chivalry,' said Holyoake,
'Puts angels in the wrong.'

'The newest way,' said Uncle Sam,
'To interrogate the brutes
Is a wet wire on the private parts
That half-electrocutes –
Though I do hate having to wash
Their vomit from my boots.'

'Don't talk so loud!' groaned Holyoake –
'We'll want the churches' votes.'

'I'm a simple chap,' sighed Holyoake,
'Politics hurt my head;
But why do you scrap with China
To the tune of a million dead
And sign a Pact with Russia,
When both of them are Red?'

'Get with it, Keith,' said Uncle Sam,
'We need the East for trade.'

'I'm a simple chap,' said Holyoake,
'Politics frighten me;
But whether it's frozen meat or men
We send across the sea,
We want good prices for our veal –
What can you guarantee?'

'Just name your price,' said Uncle Sam,
'And leave the rest to me.'

## The Gunner's Lament

### (for my wife, Te Kare)

A Maori gunner lay dying
In a paddyfield north of Saigon,
And he said to his pakeha cobber,
'I reckon I've had it, man!

'And if I could fly like a bird
To my old granny's whare
A truck and a winch would never drag
Me back to the Army.

'A coat and a cap and a well-paid job
Looked better than shovelling metal,
And they told me that Te Rauparaha
Would have fought in the Vietnam battle.

'On my last leave the town swung round
Like a bucket full of eels.
The girls liked the uniform
And I liked the girls.

'Like a bullock to the abattoirs
In the name of liberty
They flew me with a hangover
Across the Tasman Sea,

'And what I found in Vietnam
Was mud and blood and fire,
With the Yanks and the Reds taking turns
At murdering the poor,

'And I saw the reason for it
In a Viet Cong's blazing eyes –
We fought for the crops of kumara
And they are fighting for rice.

'So go and tell my sweetheart
To get another boy
Who'll cuddle her and marry her
And laugh when the bugles blow,

'And tell my youngest brother
He can have my shotgun
To fire at the ducks on the big lagoon,
But not to aim it at a man,

'And tell my granny to wear black
And carry a willow leaf,
Because the kid she kept from the cold
Has eaten a dead man's loaf,

'And go and tell Keith Holyoake
Sitting in Wellington,
However long he scrubs his hands
He'll never get them clean.'

## The Lion Skin

The old man with a yellow flower on his coat
Came to my office, climbing twenty-eight steps,
With a strong smell of death about his person
From the caves of the underworld.
The receptionist was troubled by his breath
Understandably.
              Not every morning tea break
Does Baron Saturday visit his parishioners
Walking stiffly, strutting almost,
With a cigar in his teeth – she might have remembered
Lying awake as if nailed by a spear
Two nights ago, with the void of her life
Glassed in a dark window – but suitably enough
She preferred to forget it.
                        I welcomed him
And poured him a glass of cherry brandy,
Talked with him for half an hour or so,

Having need of his strength, the skin of a dead lion,
In the town whose ladders are made of coffin wood.

The flower on his coat blazed like a dark sun.


## On Possessing the Burns Fellowship 1966

*(to Nicholas Zissermann)*

Trees move slowly. The rain drops arrows
As on the Spartans from the Persian bowstring
Some while ago, across the tennis court
Behind the convent they hope to pull down,

And I who wrote in '62,
*Dear ghosts, let me abandon*
*What cannot be held against*
*Hangmen and educators, the city of youth! –*

Drink fresh percolated coffee, lounging
In the new house, at the flash red kitchen table,
A Varsity person, with an office
Just round the corner – what nonsense!

If there is any culture here
It comes from the black south wind
Howling above the factories
A handsbreadth from Antarctica,

Whatever the architect and planner
Least understand – not impossibly the voice
Of an oracle rising from that
Old battered green veranda

Beyond the board fence: a blood transfusion
From the earth's thick veins! As if
Caesar had died, and clouds, leaves, conspired to make
A dark mocking funeral wreath.


## The Kraken

Where the sighing combs of water
Talk under broken jetties, and the long

84

Green flats of weed that Heaphy painted
Wait for the withheld kiss of the tide,

You who stroll on cliff-top boulders and
The abandoned gun-pit, do not

Expect the sea to break its own laws,
Or any Venus to be born

Out of the gulf's throat. Even the dead
Who made from this dug earth, proud air,

Something cruder than they meant,
Hang on museum walls. As night comes

You will hear from the lighthouse the foghorn speak
With a shuddering note, and watch how the kraken's wide

Blinding tendrils move like smoke
Over the rock neck, the muttering flats, the houses.


## The Inflammable Woman

It was plain to see the sense of being a woman
Troubled her. She sat on the edge of the sofa
Holding a glass of gin and fizz
With seeds floating, trying to look at ease
Though the conversation about God and Kafka
Bored her to the core . . . What core? What did she most
Regard herself as being? (Though no one
Bothered to find out) – a white rose? an old stocking?
An animal dying of hunger?
                                        The host
Offered her another gin. He did not
Notice something rather shocking:
That the sofa was slowly turning to ash
Though keeping its shape. And then the leg of a table,
Part of the carpet, a corkscrew, went first red hot
Then a metallic grey. The toe of my shoe
Was nibbled away in a flash
(She, poor woman, all the while
Gripping her glass and hoping the party would not be long) –
I wondered what to do,

Whether to ring the Fire Brigade or smile
And put the whole occasion into a fable
As I finally did, being no longer young,
And carrying always a private bucket of sand. Thank you.


## The Maori Jesus

I saw the Maori Jesus
Walking on Wellington Harbour.
He wore blue dungarees.
His beard and hair were long.
His breath smelt of mussels and paraoa.
When he smiled it looked like the dawn.
When he broke wind the little fishes trembled.
When he frowned the ground shook.
When he laughed everybody got drunk.

The Maori Jesus came on shore
And picked out his twelve disciples.
One cleaned toilets in the Railway Station;
His hands were scrubbed red to get the shit out of
        the pores.
One was a call-girl who turned it up for nothing.
One was a housewife who'd forgotten the Pill
And stuck her TV set in the rubbish can.
One was a little office clerk
Who'd tried to set fire to the Government Buildings.
Yes, and there were several others;
One was an old sad quean;
One was an alcoholic priest
Going slowly mad in a respectable parish.

The Maori Jesus said, 'Man,
From now on the sun will shine.'

He did no miracles;
He played the guitar sitting on the ground.

The first day he was arrested
For having no lawful means of support.
The second day he was beaten up by the cops
For telling a dee his house was not in order.
The third day he was charged with being a Maori
And given a month in Mount Crawford.
The fourth day he was sent to Porirua
For telling a screw the sun would stop rising.

The fifth day lasted seven years
While he worked in the asylum laundry
Never out of the steam.
The sixth day he told the head doctor,
'I am the Light in the Void;
I am who I am.'
The seventh day he was lobotomized;
The brain of God was cut in half.

On the eighth day the sun did not rise.
It didn't rise the day after.
God was neither alive nor dead.
The darkness of the Void,
Mountainous, mile-deep, civilized darkness
Sat on the earth from then till now.


## A View from Duffy's Farm

The door is all but broken;
there's air and space inside, and
no one's likely to come in

with a telegraphed demand
for love, opinions, money,
because the high lip of ground

belonged once to Matt Duffy
and now to the wind that blows
this way over the south sea

carrying a whiff of ice,
the farm's first owner. The stove
rusty; the sink dry – my shoes

crunch the dirt that 'possums leave
in a farmhouse that's been long
abandoned. Yet one could live

quite well on almost nothing
in this place – some turnips from
a neighbour's field – gathering

mussels from the rocks . . . *Too grim*,
you think? I'd sew up the old
burst mattress in the bedroom

where Sarah slept . . . Sarah filled
a hedge-gap in Duffy's life,
perhaps more as a burnt child

than as a *de facto* wife:
drunk, she would give it away
to a man well heeled enough

to buy a drink. Quietly
with one belt on the earhole
Duffy the husband would say,

'Get in the truck!' Too simple . . .
Soon after she was buried,
on a bus he said, for all

to hear, spreading his arms wide
as if to grip some woman
of air – 'She died like a bird

in the frost' – No ghost, no one
will haunt here, because the door
is mercifully broken

as hearts, lives, rocks break. Down there
under twisted apple trees
that bear no fruit, a river

seems to bend the heads of grass
running invisibly through
the crooked gully. It flows

winter and summer down to
the beach, the township, as if
it ran from a hole in the clay

that Duffy had dug. *Belief*
is not the name for it . . . Let
the mind rest, the hard weight of

knowledge drop, as winter light
glitters on brown thistle-heads
outside the door: I cannot

promise more than this, the clods
divided by purgation
of frost, rustling autumn heads

of thistle – space, air, light in
a room whose door is broken.

## The River

Nothing as broad as
the river can be seen
these days: it was dark
brown and deep
at corners where cattle graze,

and ran silently
by Mackenzie's cottage
where he made his boats
at its edge
choosing the thwarts cunningly

from bent manuka,
and we'd paddle upstream
past the ducks' island
in a dome
of daylong silence never

to be broken – I
break it now! The river
is foul weed and sludge
narrower
than I had supposed, fed by

a thousand drains: thus
the heart is twisted free
by thought's knife: the creek
runs to sea
finding its way without us.

## Words to Lay a Strong Ghost

### (after Catullus)

### 1 The Party

A kind of cave – still on the brandy,
And coming in from outside,
I didn't like it – the room like a tunnel
And everybody gassing in chairs –

Or count on finding you there, smiling
Like a stone Diana at
Egnatius' horse-laugh – not my business exactly
That he cleans his teeth with AJAX,

But he's the ugliest South Island con man
Who ever beat up a cripple . . .
*Maleesh* – the booze rolls back, madam;
I'm stuck here in the void

Looking at my journey's end –
Two breasts like towers – the same face
That brought Troy crashing
Down like a chicken coop – black wood and flames!


## 8 *The Wound*

It is not women only
Who lose themselves in the wound of love –
When Attis ruled by Cybele
Tore out his sex with a flint knife,

He became a girl. Blood fell
In flecks on the black forest soil –
So it was for me, Pyrrha,
And the wound will ache, aches now,

Though I hear the flute-players
And the rattling drum. To live in
Exile from the earth I came from,
Pub, bed, table, a fire of hot bluegum,

The boys in the bathing sheds playing cards –
It's hard to live on Mount Ida
Where frost bites the flesh
And the sun stabs at the roots of trees,

No longer a man – Ah! don't let
Your lion growl and run against me,
Cybele's daughter – I accept
Hard bondage, harder song!

## 12 *The Rock*

Arms of Promethean rock
Thrust out on either
Side of a bare white strip
Of wave-ridged sand – long before

I ever met you, Pyrrha,
The free world held me in its heart,
And half my grief is only
The grief of a child torn from the breast

Who remembers – who cannot forget
The shielding arms of a father,
Maybe Poseidon – out there
Where the waves never cease to break

In the calmest weather, there's a hump-backed
Jut of reef – we called it Lion Rock –
Growling with its wild white mane
As if it told us even then

Death is the one door out of the labyrinth!
Not your fault – to love, hate, die,
Is natural – as under quick sand-grains
The broken bladders lie.

## 13 *The Flower*

They've bricked up the arch, Pyrrha,
That used to lead into
Your flat on Castle Street – Lord, how
I'd pound the kerb for hours,

Turning this way and that
Outside it, like a hooked fish
Wanting the bait but not the barb –
Or else a magnetized needle!

Well; they've bricked it up – fair
Enough! You've sunk your roots in Australia,
And I'm free to write verses,
Grow old, be married, watch my children clutter

*Their* lives up . . . It was always a tomb,
That place of yours! I didn't know
Then how short life is – how few
The ones who really touch us

Right at the quick – I'm a successful
Man of letters, Pyrrha –
Utterly stupid! – a forty-year-old baby
Crying out for a lost nurse

Who never cared much. The principle
That should have made me tick went early
Half underground, as at the paddock's edge
You'll see in autumn some flower

(Let's say a dandelion)
Go under the farmer's boots
Like a faded sun
Cut with a spade.


## To my Father in Spring

Father, the fishermen go
down to the rocks at twilight
when earth in the undertow

of silence is drowning, yet
they tread the bladdered weedbeds
as if death and life were but

the variation of tides –
while you in your garden shift
carefully the broken sods

to prop the daffodils left
after spring hail. You carry
a kerosene tin of soft

bread and mutton bones to the
jumping hens that lay their eggs
under the bushes slily –

not always firm on your legs
at eighty-four. Well, father,
in a world of bombs and drugs

you charm me still – no other
man is quite like you! That smile
like a low sun on water

tells of a cross to come. Shall
I eavesdrop when Job cries out
to the Rock of Israel?

No; but mourn the fishing net
hung up to dry, and walk with
you the short track to the gate

where crocuses lift the earth.


## At the Franz Josef Glacier

The hot rust-coloured springs in the riverbed
Were dry, but a smell of sulphur

Haunted the trees along the faultline
Under the glacier face where the guide

Split with his ice axe a boulder of cunninghamite
And showed us the small rock garnets

Like blood drops. Brunner wrote of this country:
'March is a bad month to ford the rivers

On account of the moss that grows . . .' Yes, explorer,
Deerstalker, have to pass the needle's eye

To get where they are going. The griefs I carry
Are nothing. All men die. What sign

Can I leave on cairn or tree to tell
The next comer that my thoughts were human?

As red moss grows on the glacial stone,
Then thicker spores whose acid crumbles it

A little – then the seeds the birds may drop,
Making their own earth, sending down roots,

Cracking and rending the rock – so may my words
Give shade in a land that lacks a human heart.

93

## At the Fox Glacier Hotel

One kind of love, a Tourist Bureau print
Of the Alps reflected in Lake Matheson

(Turned upside down it would look the same)
Smiles in the dining room, a lovely mirror

For any middle-aged Narcissus to drown in –
I'm peculiar; I don't want to fall upwards

Into the sky! Now, as the red-eyed tough
West Coast beer-drinkers climb into their trucks

And roar off between colonnades
Of mossed rimu, I sit for a while in the lounge

In front of a fire of end planks
And wait for bedtime with my wife and son,

Thinking about the huge ice torrent moving
Over bluffs and bowls of rock (some other

Kind of love) at the top of the valley –
How it might crack our public looking-glass

If it came down to us, jumping
A century in twenty minutes,

So that we saw, out of the same window
Upstairs where my underpants are hanging to dry,

Suddenly – no, not ourselves
Reflected, or a yellow petrol hoarding,

But the other love, yearning over our roofs
Black pinnacles and fangs of toppling ice.


## Mother and Son

### 1

Blowflies dive-bomb the sitting-room
Table, this dry spring morning,

94

In my mother's house. As I did in my 'teens,
I listen again to the Roman-lettered clock

Chiming beside the statue of Gandhi
Striding towards God without any shadow

Along the mantelpiece. Time is a spokeless wheel.
Fantails have built a nest on the warm house wall

Among the passion vines. The male one lurks.
The female spreads her fan. Out in the rock garden

White-headed my mother weeds red polyanthus,
Anemone, Andean crocus,

And the gold and pearl trumpets called angels' tears.
Mother, I can't ever wholly belong

In your world. What if the dancing fantail
Should hatch tomorrow a dragon's egg?

Mother, in all our truces of the heart
I hear the pearl-white angels musically weeping.


2


There's more to it. Those wood-framed photographs
Also beside the clock, contain your doubtful angels,

My brother with hair diagonally brushed
Over his forehead, with a hot dark eye,

And myself, the baby blondish drowsing child
So very slow to move away from the womb!

Saddled and ridden to Iceland and back by the night-hag
He learnt early that prayers don't work, or work

After the need has gone. Mother, your son
Had gained a pass degree in Demonology

Before he was twelve – how else can you make a poet? –
Yet we're at one in the Catholic Church.

I go out to meet you. Someone is burning weeds
Next door. The mother fantail flutters

95

Chirping with white eyebrows and white throat
On a branch of lawsoniana, and the darting

Father bird comes close when I whisper to him
With a susurrus of the tongue.

## At Kuri Bush

A few days back I climbed the mound
Where the farmhouse had stood,

As green as any that the Maoris made
Along that coast. The fog was blowing

Through gates and up gullies
Hiding even the stems of cocksfoot grass

That had sprung up in place of
The sitting-room table and the small brass

Kerosene lamp my mother lighted
Every night, whose white wick would burn

Without changing colour. Somebody must have
Used the old brushwood fence for kindling

Twenty years ago. Outside it
My father stood when I was three or less,

Holding me up to look at
The gigantic rotating wheel of the stars

Whose time isn't ours. The mound yielded
No bones, no coins, but only

A chip of the fallen chimney
I put in the pocket of a damp coat

Before I bumbled back down to the road
With soaking trousers. That splinter of slate

Rubbed by keys and cloth like an amulet
Would hold me back if I tried to leave this island

For the streets of London or New York.
I hope one day they'll plant me in

The kind of hole they dig for horses
Under a hilltop cabbage tree

Not too far from the river that goes
Southwards to the always talking sea.

## The Bridge

Far up the creek I
often rode in
a rented canoe, my
paddles barely touching
the water's pollen dusted skin

where gorse-pods floated,
and slid under
the Black Bridge's rusted
bolts and tarry roof: there
one could make sherbert from water

with a matchbox full
of fizzing fine
powder. It tasted well,
nipping the tongue, in high
summer, when crickets chirred at noon

on each bush – lately
I went that way
not thinking, and saw the
bridge under fifty bull-
dozed yards of gravel and dry clay.

## The Titan

The rock limbs of Prometheus
Lie twisted at the entrance of the bay;
Like corroded iron, overgrown
By barnacle, periwinkle and sea-lichen.
Children who bathe in that place clamber
Timidly over the ridges of his shoulder

Bull-wrinkled, spray-moistened, brushed by the kiss
Of the south wind that blows this way
Five hundred leagues from the breasts of the Andes
Over sterile beds of foam. Think:

It is a long time since he brought
The fire of Zeus to us,

Lightening our chaos. For many aeons
Hour by hour the sea vulture
Has been tearing at his guts. We had
All but forgotten his pain and his gift.
Calamity, time, deeply thwarted desire,
Bring us again to the place of the dark Titan,

And there are others. I cannot hear their voices.
I cannot see their faces. Not even the jingle
Of a stirrup, as they cross the river mouth
In late evening when sandflies rise
From rotted kelp. Only a pressure at
The fences of the mind. From clay mounds they gathe
To share the Titan's blood with us.

## Fitz Drives Home the Spigot

When you hammered the spigot in, Fitz,
With blow after blow of a mallet,
I felt the town shudder, very much afraid
That the drunk man would be king,

That the meticulous sorrow
Of widows and spinsters with small zip purses
Would be disregarded by drunken coalmen
Pissing against the hedge,

That daughters would go down singing in droves
To the oil tankers and open their white legs
To rough-handed rum-fed sailors, that well-bred sons
Would dive in your great barrel and happily drown,

That the black bones of Dionysus
Buried under the Fire Assurance Building
Had sprouted a million wild green vines
Cracking the pavements and the gravestones –

But fortunately you did not strike too hard!
The town shook once, and then regained its proper
Monotonous man-killing identity,
While you rubbed your belly and drank one pony beer.

## At Rakiura

You may be sure no matron will ever row out
To get a child by sitting on the snouted rock

At the centre of the harbour. That phallic monster is
Of danger only to the seaplane

Taxi-ing in past the wooden lighthouse
Where muttonbirds squawk in their burrows

Growing fat for the Maori. No mitigation
Of the sense of being trapped by life

Will come to us from the shelves of the museum
Where they've stacked the junk of the early days,

Bullets, clay pipes, paper money,
The Lord's Prayer written on a seashell.

But honeymooners may sponge out a quarrel
With a kiss that gathers half its meaning

From beaches where the surf bangs over
Like the cracking of a two-mile-long flax whip,

And we who are older look at the headstones of
The grim dead, as ignorant as ourselves,

Those whom the cold Strait or whisky killed,
And go back to the guesthouse to stretch out

And hear the chug of a generator
Or the monotonous rumble of the wind above

The high roof, not talking, just lying
And thinking of nothing on a sagging bed

That would extend (I imagine) an equal tolerance
To a paying guest or a moneyless suicide.

## Winter River

Nothing is colder than this water in winter
when winds crack the lopped pines
on the Domain bank and send cones
rolling down to the water . . .

Thick bare brown roots tangled
below the sod wall. The boys
and their girls would sit on Saturdays
in a fog of awkwardness and watch

the river run out to the bay.
Ah well – it's easy
to come back, more or less alive
inside one's own unbreakable

glass dome, a dying Martian,
and think about youth.
I never liked it much.
I did not venture

to touch the thick blonde matted curls
of those man-swallowing dolls, our big sisters.
I had no sister.
Their giggles made me tremble

and coast away to the bathing shed latrine
in itchy summer torpor,
furiously inventing a unicorn
who hated the metal of Venus.

Yet they weren't metal. Now
they sag on porches, in back rooms,
flabby as I am, and the river
carries a freight of floating pine cones.


## Grandfather

Old and
bald-headed as a turtle,
I remember you,
grandfather, at the trembling kitchen range –

(all your hopes drawn in
to a pond where the light
flickered and gripped you from above,
your dead wife's love) –

so hot with the damper out
a match would flare
at a touch of its explosive tip
on the black glossy surface!

Ah yes – you'd take
the white bone chanter
down from its rack, finger it and play it
so sweetly, lightly, the wristbone of a man

hollow at each end, or so
I think of it, life measured
into a tube wound round
with bands of silver.

You'd caught the notes, you'd stolen them
long ago, sitting like a young
ferret in a flaxbush while your father
tried to teach the elder son.

He taught you then. A champion piper
you could never read a note,
you *were* the tune! It didn't
help you much

when the bailiffs were in,
and the butcher of God's Word
dragged you in half, much later,
so that you gave up smoking and whisky,

fell, rose, fell, rose, fell,
always a worry to your wife –
my looking-glass twin,
when the fumes were boiling in your head

on a black morning, the horses stamping
unfed, the manuka dripping
in gullies mortgaged to the hilt,
did you say '*I* am Hell'?

I salute whatever
burns, our brother Lucifer
raging! This I understand.
Never the unhurt quiet end.


## The Girl in the Bookshop

The sadness of the girl in the bookshop
Belongs to autumn and its leagues of sky
That quench all thought, or else those crackling leaves
That turn to powder when you grind them
Between the finger and the thumb. Observe
The small breasts uplifted, the mouth without lipstick
Tightening a little as she fits in the slot
Of the till one dirty ten-dollar note:
Something behind the mind is not
Alive. Plates piled in a cold kitchen
Facing a brick wall where the spider weaves
Unintelligible scrollwork! – her wishes – she has need of
A lover made of bread and gelignite
To caress those modest legs, or to be invaded by
A singing raingod; but rather
We have given her over to Winter
Riding her way on a horse of wind and ice,
His beard full of twigs, each eye an open grave,
Who will pick her up in arms that have
The knotted veins of an old ploughman
And carry her into the deep caves
Of that security we also die in.


## At Naseby

'Mountains are mothers' – I wrote
those three words in an MS.
book, beside a new poem,
long ago with a pen cut
from a rooster feather, when
the earth and I were much less

compatible    living then
in a lean-to at the side
of a sun-dried-brick cottage
a yard or two up the road
where they've put a FOR SALE sign –
no bigger than a garage,

but it's the place that counts – I
must have been mad! There are no
mountains here; just the poplars
raining down orange leaves to
rot in ditches, and a spry
shop that sells bread, potatoes,

chutney, magazines – far off
on the skyline a small spoor
of hills, but nearer at hand
nothing apart from the moth-
bright family baches and
sod houses worn by weather

shapeless as graves, among which
water-courses ramble like
veins of memory. I'm not
haunted much, climbing the track
to the swimming-dam, by that
grim boy step by step at watch,

my judge below the larches,
his mind like a coiled spring wound
tight by dread and hope, a quill
tucked in his pocket – because
I have forgotten his wound,
and trudging towards nightfall

I find that whatever is
other than self sleeps now like
a wife at my elbow, with
rough breasts of stone, from whose kiss
I turn, so as not to break
the hymen of Sister Death.


### Winter Sea

I remember, much too early
To see it clearly through the dark lens,
My grandmother among the roses
An old woman with red cheeks – and how she
      slowly built
A ball of silver paper to stand in the never-opened
Dust-proof cabinet below the painting of horses
Running away from lightning.
                    There was a smell

Of coldness in the house and a child could touch
The china jug and basin in the bedroom
Cold and rough to the fingers, or see without stooping
Beyond the veranda a blue cold garden
Through a pane of coloured glass.
                              No doubt her hands were warm.

She carried a sack of oatmeal on her back
Twelve miles, walking beside the breakers
From the town to her own gate. At least once it must have
     happened that a blinding sheet
Of spray rose from the winter waves to cover her.

I go down to the beach and watch the fishermen casting
Their lines out beyond the evening surf.
These men stow tackle in the boots of cars.
Their lead sinkers catch in the crevices of rocks.
No names. No ancestors. The sea stands
Upright like the walls of an empty grave.


## Reflections at Lowburn Ferry

They take trucks on board for the river crossing.
Not always safe. It has been known to happen
That the ferry tipped and the truck slid back
Slowly into the Clutha with ten men cursing
And three men praying that the stuck
Cab door would shift. But the willows are green
Low down on the water. I've often thought that when
I finally flake, or a minute after, the gate will open
On this damned ferry. Very likely they won't have heard
Of Good Pope John. They will ask me why
I have no obol under my tongue,
Or a cent, or a penny – unless the price has risen –
And I will float in the mud like an old sad turd,
Never to live, never to die,
Wishing to Christ that Christ would come along,
Even the Protestant Christ, like Oscar Wilde when young,
To shake a tambourine with the souls in prison.


## Winter Poem to my Wife

Because the fog is a curtain over the town
Because the lights are rare and few like virgins

Because the fire spits little sparks and weeps white resin,
Because I am a wooden husband,

You go away from me down to the roots of water
To find the spiny sea-egg
Whose yolk breaks molten in the mouth,
You go down to the sea gate
And gather the black pods of iron flax!

Because the trees are fur on an old hairy cat
Because the cars travel with windmills in their bellies
Because the houses are shaking their crumbling fists of mildew,
Because I am a warty husband,

You go away from me into the Maori church
To find an old bone flute
Playing by itself in the darkest corner
And the shark's tooth and the flounder
And the tears of the albatross!

I accept these journeys.

Because the wind has lost its powder keg
Because the frost has started to scythe the street
Because the moon is a blind wet crystal,
Because I am a silent husband,

You go away from me to the middle of the bush
To find a coat of stones and staples
Or the lifted hair of the hurricane
That tries to spin the sun in a new direction.
That's not a bad idea.

I accept my fate.


## A Small Ode on Mixed Flatting

*Elicited by the decision of the
Otago University authorities to
forbid this practice among students*

Dunedin nights are often cold
(I notice it as I grow old);
The south wind scourging from the Pole
Drives every rat to his own hole,
Lashing the drunks who wear thin shirts

And little girls in mini-skirts.
Leander, that Greek lad, was bold
To swim the Hellespont raging cold
To visit Hero in her tower
Just for an amorous half-hour,
And lay his wet brine-tangled head
Upon her pillow – Hush! The dead
Can get good housing – Thomas Bracken,
Smellie, McLeod, McColl, McCracken,
A thousand founding fathers lie
Well roofed against the howling sky
In mixed accommodation – Hush!
It is the living make us blush
Because the young have wicked hearts
And blood to swell their private parts.
To think of corpses pleases me;
They keep such perfect chastity.
O Dr Williams, you were right
To shove the lovers out of sight;
Now they can wander half the night
Through coffee house and street and park
And fidget in the dripping dark,
While we play Mozart and applaud
The angel with the flaming sword!
King Calvin in his grave will smile
To know we know that man is vile;
But Robert Burns, that sad old rip
From whom I got my Fellowship
Will grunt upon his rain-washed stone
Above the empty Octagon,
And say – 'O that I had the strength
To slip yon lassie half a length!
Apollo! Venus! Bless my ballocks!
Where are the games, the hugs, the frolics?
Are all you bastards melancholics?
Have you forgotten that your city
Was founded well in bastardry
And half your elders (God be thankit)
Were born the wrong side of the blanket?
You scholars, throw away your books
And learn your songs from lasses' looks
As I did once – ' Ah, well; it's grim;
But I will have to censor him.
He liked to call a spade a spade
And toss among the glum and staid
A poem like a hand grenade –
And I remember clearly how

(Truth is the only poet's vow)
When my spare tyre was half this size,
With drumming veins and bloodshot eyes
I blundered through the rain and sleet
To dip my wick in Castle Street,
Not on the footpath – no, in a flat,
With a sofa where I often sat,
Smoked, drank, cursed, in the company
Of a female student who unwisely
Did not mind but would pull the curtain
Over the window – And did a certain
Act occur? It did. It did.
As Byron wrote of Sennacherib –
'The Assyrian came down like a wolf on the fold
And his cohorts were gleaming in purple and gold' –
But now, at nearly forty-two,
An inmate of the social zoo,
Married, baptized, well heeled, well shod,
Almost on speaking terms with God,
I intend to save my moral bacon
By fencing the young from fornication!
Ah, Dr Williams, I agree
We need more walls at the Varsity;
The students who go double-flatting
With their she-catting and tom-catting
Won't ever get a pass in Latin;
The moral mainstay of the nation
Is careful, private masturbation;
A vaseline jar or a candle
Will drive away the stink of scandal!
The Golden Age will come again –
Those tall asthenic bird-like men
With spectacles and lecture notes,
Those girls with wool around their throats
Studying till their eyes are yellow
A new corrupt text of *Othello*,
Vaguely agnostic, rationalist,
A green banana in each fist
To signify the purity
Of educational ecstasy –
And, if they marry, they will live
By the Clinical Imperative:
A car, a fridge, a radiogram,
A clean well-fitted diaphragm,
Two-and-a-half children per
Family; to keep out thunder
Insurance policies for each;

A sad glad fortnight at the beach
Each year, when Mum and Dad will bitch
From some old half-forgotten itch –
Turn on the lights! – or else the gas!
If I kneel down like a stone at Mass
And wake my good wife with bad dreams,
And scribble verse on sordid themes,
At least I know man was not made
On the style of a slot-machine arcade –
Almost, it seems, the other day,
When Francis threw his coat away
And stood under the palace light
Naked in the Bishop's sight
To marry Lady Poverty
In folly and virginity,
The angels laughed – do they then weep
Tears of blood if two should sleep
Together and keep the cradle warm?
Each night of earth, though the wind storm,
Black land behind, white sea in front,
Leander swims the Hellespont;
To Hero's bed he enters cold;
And he will drown; and she grow old –
But what they tell each other there  .
You'll not find in a book anywhere.

## To Mate With

To mate with the air is difficult –
That sinuous invisible creature
Blows hot, blows cold, rubbing her grit of pollen
On the bodies of ploughmen and mountaineers

Who itch and curse! To mate with a river
Or a filled-up miner's quarry, that pleases me;
My cold kind mother, Sister Water,
Has no comment, accepts whatever I am,

Yet one may think of tentacles
Reaching, searching from under the darkest ledge,
And not want to be married. To mate with rock
Is obvious, fatal, and what man was made for,

Whose heart of rock trembles like a magnet
For deserts, graves, any hole in the ground

Where he may hide from Zeus. To mate with fire
Is what the young want most, like salamanders

Weeping in solitary flame, embracing
Red-hot stoves, walking the lava crust
An inch away from fire. Then, my old gravedigger,
To mate with a woman is the choice

Containing all other kinds of death –
Fire, water, rock, and the airy succubus,
Without parable, without consolation
Except that each is the other's boulder and victim.


## The Flame

My son sleeps above – my wife is sleeping also –
My son's room smells of the incense that he burns
Before the Buddha – as good a way as any
Of yoking the demons that rise at puberty,

Not demons, other selves. At 4 a.m. I still sit
Awake at the kitchen table
Like a Martian in a space suit
Drinking coffee and writing. In forty years

I haven't found a cure
For being human. I can't get drunk
Now as I used to, dowsing the flame with whisky;
I have to live and burn

Thinking of Christ – Christ, who is all men
Yet has to be discovered
By each on his own – not this morning
His blood only, but his resurrection,

Like the voice of the wind blowing on troubled waves,
Like hard buds of japonica,
Christ who is ointment, and for whom I carry
The incurable wound of life, and stand in the black flame.


## The Instruments

If this were indeed the final night
High up on the hill, above the gold claims,
Where wet needles fall on the shoulders,

Where voices out of the ground compel
Pity and recognition – if this night were final,
A drawing down of blinds

Over the human face and the instruments of torture,
I could understand it.
                    But not yet; one must still go
Another journey to another place
Where without kisses, without the clasping of fingers,
The snake-haired women will appear
Naked, clothed in our own deformity,

And take us singly through the gate in the rock
To the paddock of the slavegirl Blandina,
To where the soul is broken or else becomes
A bird, born out of blood, another creature.


## The Fear of Change

If you and I were woken suddenly
By the drums of Revolution in the street –
Or suppose the door shot open, and there stood
Upright and singing a young bullfighter

With a skin of rough wine, offering to each of us
Death, sex, hope – or even just an
Earthquake, making the trees thrash, the roofs tumble,
Calling us loudly to consider God –

Let us admit, with no shame whatever,
We are not that kind of people;
We have learnt to weigh each word like an ounce
    of butter;
Our talent is for anger and monotony –

Therefore we will survive the singers,
The fighters, the so-called lovers – we will bury them
Regretfully, and spend a whole wet Sunday
Arguing whether the corpses were dressed in black
    or red.


## Rhadamanthus

We got to that place by an unexpected tunnel
Where the cliff top sank in a V – behind a hummock

Under the green starlike leaves
Of some plant that clings to the earth.
Venus came over the sea to us
Lying (as so many do)
In one another's arms. She left us
Like shards of a dish the spade jars on.

To love at all is to be haunted
As stones are haunted by the ghost of water
Where a creek ran once.
                              I came after twenty years
To the same place. My bones cold and heavy.
It was not wise to come back.
Boulders and clay had fallen. From some cleft
A pigeon scuttered out. Above the place of love
The cliff was a high stone Rhadamanthus
Washed by the black froth of the sea.


## Summer 1967

Summer brings out the girls in their green dresses
Whom the foolish might compare to daffodils,
Not seeing how a dead grandmother in each one governs
    her limbs,
Darkening the bright corolla, using her lips to speak through,
Or that a silver torque was woven out of
The roots of wet speargrass.
                              The young are mastered by the Dead,
Lacking cunning. But on the beaches, under the clean wind
That blows this way from the mountains of Peru,
Drunk with the wind and the silence, not moving an inch
As the surf-swimmers mount on yoked waves,
One can begin to shake with laughter,
Becoming oneself a metal Neptune.
                              To want nothing is
The only possible freedom. But I prefer to think of
An afternoon spent drinking rum and cloves
In a little bar, just after the rain had started, in another time
Before we began to die – the taste of boredom on the tongue
Easily dissolving, and the lights coming on –
With what company? I forget.
                              Where can we find the right
Herbs, drinks, bandages to cover
These lifelong intolerable wounds?
Herbs of oblivion, they lost their power to help us
The day that Aphrodite touched her mouth to ours.

## The Millstones

I do not expect you to like it. Winter
Has found his way into the tunnels of the mind
And will not leave us.
                                   Often between the millstones,
In a stranger's house, perhaps drunk,
One of us would remember
The lagoons and the water birds, sleep that came
Like the travelling of the tide under a boat's keel.

Endlessly in memory I followed the river
To the place it sprang from, among broom bushes
In a gully above the dam. Brother,
It taught me nothing but how to die;
The house is empty. In the paddock alongside it
On a tree one bitter shrunken apple.
It is the hour of ghosts.
                                   Do not forget
The time between the millstones was a real time;
The battles were real, foul sweat, foul blood,
Though now the earth is trying to persuade us
We are children again. The gales of the south sea
Will hammer tonight on a shut window.


## The Bluegums

### (for Patric Carey)

The harsh Latin word, 'reality',
Has never suited us. It means this iron sea,
These hills cleft like an anvil, no chariots, only graves.
I suggest a compromise. So that, perhaps, if one man were to die,
Then later, after the funeral, when the powdered sponge-cake had
     been cut
And set on a cane table out on the veranda,
Then if his friend were talking even about sheep or football
You would hear continuously in the pauses between the words
The first man talking in another language
As the wind does between the branches of the great gumtrees –
Or as when a boat is being launched, the furrow lengthens on the sand
And the waves steadily resound on the timbers
While somebody in an overcoat is watching –
Or if on a dead Sunday the key turns in the door
And another friend comes in, smiling a little,
Carrying a pack of cards and a bottle –

112

I ask no more than this. Those would be our poems;
Marks of the whip; a kind of punishment
For us who have drunk without hope the blood of Dionysus.


## The Doctrine

It was hope taught us to tell these lies on paper.
Scratch a poet and you will find
A small boy looking at his own face in water
Or an adolescent gripping imaginary lovers.
And the hope became real, not in action but in words,
Since words are more than nine-tenths of life.
We did not believe ourselves. Others believed us
Because they could not bear to live without some looking-glass.

'Are they real?' you ask – 'Did these things happen?'
My friend, I think of the soul as an amputee,
Sitting in a wheel-chair, perhaps in a sun-room
Reading letters, or in front of an open coal-range
Remembering a shearing gang – the bouts, the fights –
What we remember is never the truth;
And as for the body, what did it ever give us
But pain and limit? Freedom belongs to the mind.

That boy who went out and gazed at his face in the river
Was changed, they say, into a marvellous flower
Perpetually renewed in each Greek summer
Long after his tough companions had become old bones.
To act is to die. We ward off our death
With a murmuring of words.


## Instruction

The austere angel of the wind
Was our first instructor. He came with a breath of seaweed,
The savour of red currants, or an armful of dry grass,
Blowing our way above gardens and graves.
Drunk with sunlight, we listened
To a monotonous language, not of the ear alone,
Explaining the forms of nature.
                                        Either on the wood of the back steps
Where wolf spiders jumped after flies, or under the ngaio leaves
Round the corner of the shed. We were children then. His
    voice has changed.
The shed and the house have been pulled down.

I watch the branches of the ngaio tree tremble,
Shaking drops of water onto my coat –
It could be rain; it could be tears –

Those whom I loved as much as I shall ever love
Have joined their voices to that of the wind –
Those whom I loved as much as I shall ever love
Whom the world has turned slowly into air or stone
As I also turn.
                    If blood drops rise
To the surface of the grey bark, one should not go away.
The words are becoming a little clearer.


## Dunedin Morning

This humid morning half the town is waking
Like Jonah in the belly of the whale,

Uncertain whether the light is light or else
A delusion of the blood. I remember clearly

A friend who walked the yard in stockinged feet
Playing the bagpipes, thumbing the great drone,

With a sound like the wind in the macrocarpas. But now,
At this moment, the town climbs up from sleep,

Innocently, with a mild rumble of traffic,
As a drunkard wakes, for once, without remorse

And is glad to be alive. Surf on the beaches
This side of Black Head, like a dream remembered

For a while after waking, will haunt and comfort
Those who go to factories, offices and libraries,

Putting on the daylight mask, the hard heavy
Face of wood or lead. A susurrus of wind is moving

The fallen leaves on the ground by the museum,
As the day begins, having its own eccentric shape

Which none of us will ever know completely.

## Letter from the Mountains

There was a message. I have forgotten it.
There was a journey to make. It did not come to anything.
But these nights, my friend, under the iron roof
Of this old rabbiters' hut where the traps
Are still hanging up on nails,
Lying in a dry bunk, I feel strangely at ease.
The true dreams, those longed-for strangers,
Begin to come to me through the gates of horn.

I will not explain them. But the city, all that other life
In which we crept sadly like animals
Through thickets of dark thorns, haunted by the moisture
        of women
And the rock of barren friendship, has now another shape.
Yes, I thank you. I saw you rise like a Triton,
A great reddish gourd of flesh,
From the sofa at that last party, while your mistress smiled
That perfect smile, and shout as if drowning –
'You are always –'
                Despair is the only gift;
When it is shared, it becomes a different thing; like rock, like
        water;
And so you also can share this emptiness with me.

Tears from faces of stone. They are our own tears.
Even if I had forgotten them
The mountain that has taken my being to itself
Would still hang over this hut, with the dead and the living
Twined in its crevasses. My door has forgotten how to shut.


## The Searchers

If one were to shout from the hollow of these cliffs
Toward the black sky – if one were to cry out suddenly
As a bird might hurtle in stupidity from the ledges
Toward the heart of the storm, as if the storm were peace –
What answer?
                An echo descending, the ghost of a falling feather.
And we remember our fathers talking of this place,
How at such and such a rock the young man was drowned
Whose hair spread out like a halo, but when they dragged him
        into the boat
And turned him over, the nose and the lips had been eaten away;
How the woman tortured by love plunged into the blowhole

And was never found. We have come from elsewhere, choked by
    the tumour of life, wishing to be
Made over; and the spirits of the unwise will not haunt
Or trouble us. They are too much like ourselves.
It is perhaps that we search in the face of the storm for the
    features of a Father
Lost elsewhere; we discover a burnt tree-trunk or the bones of
    a dog;
And we are changing slowly into columns of gutted stone.


## The Black Star

I do not know when exactly we saw the black star rise
Above the mountains and fields and the places where we
Were accustomed to gather. The colour of the earth was changed
As if by mildew. It was a calm day,
If I remember rightly, with a dry wind blowing over
The fruit-bearing plateau. Blossoms were falling that day
Onto our heads, into the wine
We had set out on tables. Then a child shouted,
'Look at the black star!'
                We looked up and saw it,
A spot, a disc, a kind of hole through which
The blue water of the sky was being drained out;
Yet the sun was still there, the wind kept blowing,
The wine held its savour.
                There were a few among us
Who wept, pierced themselves with thorns, and cried,
'Deliver us, Christ, from our sin!'
                What sin?
Sins are bred in the marrow of the bones of men,
Painful no doubt, but the wisest learn to live with them.
I forgot to say some of us began to scatter paper money
On the greying earth. No one would stoop to pick it up.
The old people now keep close to their houses,
And the young have grown ungovernable – they run wild
    wearing masks
Of hair and stick and bone. The middle-aged are finding it
Tolerable; at least I do.
                As for the black star,
It whirls, it stands, it governs the day and the night,
And though we prefer not to speak about it,
We regard it in a sense as a new god – god or machine – we
    call it
The Equalizer.

## The Seals

Two boys in jeans are gathering bits of wood,
Wading in gumboots at the sea's edge;

Two dogs plunge into the yellow surf
And come out shaking their coats and spraying sticky water

Everywhere. We ourselves are treading
On the rotted cork floats of fishermen

That crumble underfoot, or else we climb
Awkwardly along these spray-dark

Ledges, gripping the chains that rasp the hand,
Pegged to the rock with rusted pins of iron,

And look for the seals. The seals have gone
Some time ago to the ice-cap in the south.

We won't find them here; instead we will return
By car on the winding road beside the mudflats,

Trying to remember – I do not know the name
To call it by; but the seals I think might have told us what it was

Before they vanished into the great mirror
Where we also travel, not by the easy death

Of water, but by land, sun-struck, moon-blinded and
Pollutedly ourselves.


## The Bargain

The rows of pea-plants in my neighbour's garden
Glisten with the dew. Paths of wet asphalt

Climb the near-by hill, under some kind of tree
Whose leaves topple in green waterfalls,

Leading very likely to a car-park or a junk-yard
But able to be thought of as the wandering track

That goes to a place where Brother Ass can bray
Without burdens. I can smoke, type letters, wind

117

The cuckoo clock, drink lukewarm coffee
In my scrubbed house – I have accepted God's bribe,

To be content with not being dead,
His singing eunuch – and my son who clatters

His hippie bells from room to room, my wife
Who makes pies out of buttered bread at the white range,

Even the grey cat blinking and curling its claws
In the armchair, are certain the bargain's a right one –

Yet if the prisoner ceased one day to sweat and rage
In his cell of jumping nerves and layered muscle,

Dreaming of wild women and guerilla battles,
Bridges blown up, farewells in African hovels,

I would not be I, and the bargain useless,
For He would be cheated of the aroma of bitter blood

Spilt on the cross-tree, and I would have become
Simply the dead man hanging, the abdicated Jesus.


## Epilogue For Ian

The subject is not to my liking,
How this one whispered – 'Bugger God' – and lay
Down dead in time to the famous tribal lament,

Or that one, having discovered the Vacuum, shrank
Rapidly to the shape of a little stone doll,
Labels that we invent and re-invent

For the same bottle. I can tell you, cousin,
Often I see my friends the suicides
Stabbing like needles through the cloth of life

To find the space behind it, or exploding
Like anxious migratory birds
That leave the pierhead empty and go north,

Counting them lucky but uncivil since
They did not want to share the fug with us in
This other death. But lately having heard

118

The great shout of judgement from your coffin
Standing on trestles in the asbestos chapel,
Preferring a bullet to a mother's kiss,

I admit I was wrong. Therefore, without argument,
While cars and relatives groan on gravel roads,
Sleep the black-bannered, the rock-undermining,

Sleep the contagious original sleep,
Now you have found the perfect girlfriend, now
The dark waters their reflections keep.


## Seances

### (for Colin Durning)

These mornings when the dead harass our lives
As children punish a dull parent,
With messages darker, wider, colder than
The crumbs of water on the sea's table,
It would be possible to let go the job
Painting or scaffolding the Tower of Babel,

Diver and dreamer, it would be easy
To cuddle up in the foetal envelope, pull
Over one's head the hummocked coverlet
Of trees and things. We have to put on instead
The space suit of money, the clean hair shirt,
That separate us from the lazy dead,

The irresponsible unborn. My brother,
I suggest we sit as usual in that café
Underground, a not too hard to bear
Grotto of the mind – talk, drink – where one can see
On certain days the stone-white face of Eurydice
Carrying in scorn her great gold helm of hair.


## The Eccentrics

It contents me to hear about them,
Not imitating their spectacular power
To bless the obstruction, master the idiot theorem:
Macpherson who rode the rapids with his arse
An inch above the water in a galloping
Canvas canoe, a lover of Scripture;

Faggott, the great drunk, who entered
A Methodist bunfight roaring like a bull
On all fours; Carmody who took pictures
Of clouds, clouds, clouds, with a tripod camera:
Giant augurs of the True, the Good, the Beautiful.

The Widow Life may weep to see them escape
The shape in the cellar, the choirboy's bellow of rape,
The whack of Caesar's whip, Queen Cybele's grip,
The excellent electrode: I condone it, Esmée,
For I admire these grey curmudgeons. They
Console me for the lover's bludgeon. May
St Ursula and the Eleven Thousand Virgins
Conduct them civilly to the Beatific Ballet.


## Ballad of the Stonegut Sugar Works

Oh in the Stonegut Sugar Works
The floors are black with grime
As I found out when I worked there
Among the dirt and slime;
I think they must have built it
In Queen Victoria's time.

I had the job of hosing down
The hoick and sludge and grit
For the sweet grains of sugar dust
That had been lost in it
For the Company to boil again
And put it on your plate;

For all the sugar in the land
Goes through that dismal dump
And all the drains run through the works
Into a filthy sump,
And then they boil it up again
For the money in each lump.

The bricks are held together by dirt
And the machines by rust
But I will work in any place
To earn myself a crust,
But work and never bow the head
As any grown man must.

And though along those slippery floors
A man might break a leg
And the foul stink of Diesel fumes
Flows through the packing shed
And men in clouds of char dust move
Like the animated dead,

To work beside your fellow men
Is good in the worst place,
To call a man your brother
And look him in the face,
And sweat and wash the sweat away
And joke at the world's disgrace.

And sweet on Auckland harbour
The waves ride in to land
Where you can sit at smoko
With the coal heaps close at hand
And watch the free white gulls a while
That on the jetty stand.

But the Clerk and the Slavedriver
Are birds of another kind,
For the clerk sits in his high glass cage
With money on his mind,
And the slavedriver down below
Can't call a slave a friend.

Instead they have (or nearly all)
The Company for a wife,
A strange kind of bedmate
That sucks away their life
On a little mad dirt track
Of chiselling and strife.

But work is work, and any man
Must learn to sweat a bit
And say politely, 'OK, mate,'
To a foreman's heavy wit,
And stir himself and only take
Five minutes for a shit.

But the sweat of work and the sweat of fear
Are different things to have;
The first is the sweat of a working man
And the second of a slave,

And the sweat of fear turns any place
Into a living grave.

When the head chemist came to me
Dressed in his white coat
I thought he might give me a medal
For I had a swollen foot
Got by shovelling rock-hard sugar
Down a dirty chute.

But no: 'I hear your work's all right,'
The chemist said to me,
'But you took seven minutes
To go to the lavatory;
I timed it with my little watch
My mother gave to me.'

'Oh thank you, thank you,' I replied
'I hope your day goes well.'
I watched the cold shark in his eye
Circling for the kill;
I did not bow the head to him
And so he wished me ill.

The foreman took another tack,
He'd grin and joke with us,
But every day he had a tale
Of sorrow for the Boss;
I did not bow the head to him
And this became this cross.

And once as he climbed the ladder
I said (perhaps unkindly) –
'I'm here to work, not drop my tweeds
At the sight of a Boss; you see,
The thing is, I'm not married
To the Sugar Company.'

As for the Company Union,
It was a tired thing;
The Secretary and Manager
Each wore a wedding ring;
They would often walk together
Picking crocuses in spring.

You will guess I got the bullet,
And it was no surprise,

For the chemists from their cages
Looked down with vulture eyes
To see if they could spot a man
Buttoning up his flies.

It's hard to take your pay and go
Up the winding road
Because you speak to your brother man
And keep your head unbowed,
In a place where the dismal stink of fear
Hangs heavy as a cloud.

The men who sweep the floors are men
(My story here must end);
But the clerk and the slavedriver
Will never have a friend;
To shovel shit and eat it
Are different in the end.

## Jerusalem Sonnets

### *(Poems for Colin Durning)*

### *1*

The small grey cloudy louse that nests in my beard
Is not, as some have called it, 'a pearl of God' –

No, it is a fiery tormentor
Waking me at two a.m.

Or thereabouts, when the lights are still on
In the houses in the pa, to go across thick grass

Wet with rain, feet cold, to kneel
For an hour or two in front of the red flickering

Tabernacle light – what He sees inside
My meandering mind I can only guess –

A madman, a nobody, a raconteur
Whom He can joke with – 'Lord,' I ask Him,

'Do You or don't You expect me to put up with lice?'
His silent laugh still shakes the hills at dawn.

## 2

The bees that have been hiving above the church porch
Are some of them killed by the rain –

I see their dark bodies on the step
As I go in – but later on I hear

Plenty of them singing with what seems a virile joy
In the apple tree whose reddish blossoms fall

At the centre of the paddock – there's an old springcart,
Or at least two wheels and the shafts, upended

Below the tree – Elijah's chariot it could be, Colin,
Because my mind takes fire a little there

Thinking of the woman who is like a tree
Whom I need not name – clumsily gripping my beads,

While the bees drum overhead and the bouncing calves look
A leather-jacketed madman set on fire by the wind.

## 3

A square picture of that old man of Ars
Whom the devil so rightly cursed as a potato-eater

Hangs on the wall not far from the foot of my bed –
Gently he smiles at me when I undo my belt

And begin to hit my back with the two brass rings
On the end of it – twenty strokes are more than enough –

Soon I climb wincing into my sleeping bag
And say to him – 'Old man, how can I,

Smoking, eating grapefruit, hack down the wall of God?'
'By love,' he answers, 'by love, my dear one,

'By love alone' – and his hippie hairdo flutters
In a wind from beyond the stars, while I stretch out and drea

Of going with Yvette in a shaky aeroplane
Across a wide black gale-thrashed sea.

## 4

The high green hill I call Mount Calvary
Is only perhaps a hundred feet high

But it fills the kitchen window – man, today I puffed
Up the sheeptrack ridges and found three posts at the top

Conveniently disposed – behind that a grove of pines
With trunks like – well, I thought of rafters, roof trees

And ocean-going canoes, nor did I pick up one
Cone or stick, thinking – 'They belong to Te Tama

'In whose breast the world is asleep' – but when I came
Back down the gully a wild calf with a

Tubular protruding eye, white
Around its edges, jerking in the socket,

Ran from me – wisely, wisely,
Smelling the master of all who is never himself.

## 5

Man, my outdoor lavatory
Has taken me three days to build –

A trench cut deep into the clay,
Then four posts, some rusty fencing wire

And a great fort of bracken
Intertwined – a noble structure

Like the gardens of Babylon, made to hide
My defecation from the eyes of the nuns –

And this morning I found a fat green frog
Squatting in the trench – I lifted him out

Against his will and set him free,
But I am trapped in the ditch of ownership

Wondering if the next gale at night
Will flatten the whole ziggurat and leave me to shit naked.

## 6

The moon is a glittering disc above the poplars
And one cloud travelling low down

Moves above the house – but the empty house beyond,
Above me, over the hill's edge,

Knotted in bramble is what I fear,
Te whare kehua — love drives, yet I draw back

From going step by step in solitude
To the middle of the Maori night

Where dreams gather – those hard steps taken one by one
Lead out of all protection, and even a crucifix

Held in the palm of the hand will not fend off
Precisely that hour when the moon is a spirit

And the wounds of the soul open – to be is to die
The death of others, having loosened the safe coat of becoming

## 7

My visitors have now departed,
Jill and Maori Johnny – they taught me to swear again

And brought me bad news of Boyle Crescent,
The junkies' pigeon-roost,

House of sorrow, house of love
To which my riderless soul night after night returns,

Neighing – 'Where are you?' It seems that somebody lit
A fire in the cellar, and two rooms were burnt out –

The wise tribe have left – Gipsy, Norma,
Yancy, Robert – the bones of my arms are aching

To hold them, my eyes want to look
On the streets of Grafton, where I was a king

For a little while – but the house of wood and straw
Is gone in smoke, and I am branded by that fire.

## 8

Many may think it out of date
That I should bend my back in a field,

Eat watercress, catch lice and pray –
'Moderation suits our time; moreover

'An educated rational approach
May set the young folk a good example

'In their adjustment' – any priest in town could tell me that;
I do not go by the priests; I go by what

My thirteen-year-old son Hoani told me
Before he left the Buddha to use a hypodermic –

'Live sparely; laugh at money;
Follow uphill the track of the bull –

'Can a snowflake exist in a raging fire?
Here are the footprints of the patriarchs.'

## 9

The crabs have returned – no creatures more communal,
Determined to be at one with their sad host,

They hang their egg-bags just above ground level
At the roots of hairs – or that is what I think

After investigation – perhaps bi-sexual,
With the double force of a mother's and a father's

Love they dig in like the troops in shellholes
Of World War One – so numerous a nation,

There's no danger, man, of genocide
Though I afflict them with pure Dettol

Time and again – I'd like to sign a truce –
'Have my moustache; and leave the rest free!'

But they have no Pope or King, Colin;
Anarchist, acephalous; they've got me stuffed!

127

## 10

Dark night – or rather, only the stars
Somebody called 'those watchfires in the sky' –

Too cold for me the thoughts of God – I crossed
The paddock on another errand,

And the cows were slow to move outside the gate
Where they sleep at night – nevertheless I came

As it were by accident into the church
And knelt again in front of the tabernacle,

His fortress – man, His thoughts are not cold!
I dare not say what fire burned then, burns now

Under my breastbone – but He came back with me
To my own house, and let this madman eat,

And shared my stupid prayer, and carried me up
As the mother eagle lifts her fluttering young with her wings

## 11

One writes telling me I am her guiding light
And my poems her bible – on this cold morning

After mass I smoke one cigarette
And hear a magpie chatter in the paddock,

The image of Hatana – he bashes at the windows
In idiot spite, shouting – 'Pakeha! You can be

'The country's leading poet' – at the church I murmured, 'Tena
To the oldest woman and she replied, 'Tena koe' –

Yet the red book is shut from which I should learn Maori
And these daft English words meander on,

How dark a light! Hatana, you have gripped me
Again by the balls, you sift and riddle my mind

On the rack of the middle world, and from my grave at length
A muddy spring of poems will gush out.

## 12

'Mother Mary Joseph Aubert, did you come here
To civilize the Maoris?' – 'No, my son,

'I came from my native France to these rough hills
Only to make them Christian' – 'Why then, mother,

'Are the corners of your mouth drawn down,
Why do you frown a little, why are your old hands folded

'In a rheumatic clench?' – 'Work, work;
Without work nobody gets to Heaven' –

'There's no work for the Maori in the towns' –
'Nonsense! There is always work, if one can

'Be tidy, chaste, well spoken' – 'The pa is all but empty,
Old woman, where you fought your fight

'And planted cherry trees – Pray for the converts' great-grandchildren
Who need drugs to sleep at night.'


## 13

It is not possible to sleep
As I did once in Grafton

Under the bright candles of a poor man's wall,
Under the delicate Japanese image

Of the Man dying whose arms embrace the night –
Lying curled in rough blankets, perhaps alone,

Perhaps not alone, with the great freedom
Of a river that runs in the dark towards its mouth –

Oh treasure of the poor, to be loved!
Arms and eyes I shall not see again –

It is not possible to sleep
The sleep of children, sweeter than marihuana,

Or to be loved so dearly as we have been loved,
With our weapons thrown down, for a breathing space.

129

## 14

I had lain down for sleep, man, when He called me
To go across the wet paddock

And burgle the dark church – you see, Colin, the nuns
Bolt the side door and I unbolt it

Like a timid thief – red light, moonlight
Mix together; steps from nowhere

Thud in the porch; a bee wakes up and buzzes;
The whole empty pa and the Maori dead

Are present – there I lie down cruciform
On the cold linoleum, a violator

Of God's decorum – and what has He to tell me?
'More stupid than a stone, what do you know

'Of love? Can you carry the weight of my Passion,
You old crab farmer?' I go back home in peace.


## 15

To give away cigarettes,
That's the hard one, Colin!

To live on rolled oats, raisins,
Potatoes, milk, raw cabbage,

It's even a pleasure – but I confess I need a smoke
More than I need a woman!

It's more like breathing – ever since I broached the guests' tobacc
(Along with the guests) I've been a doomed man!

Perhaps earlier yet – at six years old,
When I kept what I stole from my father in a rusty tin

Under the house, mixed with old rotted
Cabbage tree fibres – was it original virtue

Or original sin? I roll it now, and draw deep
The herb of darkness, preferring Nirvana to Heaven.

### 16

'Suburban street like sea of glass' –
'Plan to deafen Loch Ness monster' –

'Mayor denies link with Mafia gangsters' –
'Control that's light, fantastic, lovely,

'Under shorts or skirts' – the deaf blind world
Howling on all fours would like to deafen

Its imaginary brother, the great water lizard?
Can the Hell's Angels get to Heaven

Striding over broken teeth and glass?
Did you have your bra on, lady, when they took you to the bin?

Who is the gangster? I am only half sane
But the sane half tells me that newspapers were made

For wiping arses and covering tables,
Not for reading – now, man, I have a table cloth.

### 17

I went up barefoot to te whare kehua
This morning – but it seemed the earthquake god

Had been before me, represented by
Two young Maoris with a cunning bulldozer

That ripped up posts, earth, bramble, everything standing,
And left – well, the house

With its broken window, ghosts and lumber,
Severely out of date – I went in, treading

Carefully, to avoid a rotted kit, and knelt down
In front of the picture somebody had left to guard

The place – a cloudgazing pakeha Christ
With His heart in His hand, well felted against the weather –

And I said – 'Brother, when will your Maori church be built?
When will you hoist us all out of the graveyard?'

131

## 18

Yesterday I planted garlic,
Today, sunflowers – 'the non-essentials first'

Is a good motto – but these I planted in honour of
The Archangel Michael and my earthly friend,

Illingworth, Michael also, who gave me the seeds –
And they will turn their wild pure golden discs

Outside my bedroom, following Te Ra
Who carries fire for us in His terrible wings

(Heresy, man!) – and if He wanted only
For me to live and die in this old cottage,

It would be enough, for the angels who keep
The very stars in place resemble most

These green brides of the sun, hopelessly in love with
Their Master and Maker, drunkards of the sky.

## 19

At the centre of my mind the stone lies
And the bullock bleeds there – be it so,

Be it so, be it so,
Now and – you know, Colin,

What I mean when I say, 'Te Kare' – my life winds out
And winds back to that hard stone,

The rock of unknowing – this old bullock will kick
Once or twice, but offers himself again

To the knife of love – Te Kare, wave of the sea
On which the Dove moved before the world began,

For you I weep, for you I become a child,
Since only children have power to grip the lightning

Unharmed – by doing nothing I will do
What you desire, and bring you one day to the earthly garden.

*20*

The ring I wear on my third finger
(Alan Thornton gave me it) – one fish

For te ihi, the force of life in man;
Two fishes for Te Kare and myself,

The love of the One to the One which is the hook in our guts;
Three fishes for the Many, the cross of Te Ariki

That breaks out in flower; the anchor, te aroha –
I have worn it now, Colin, for eight months

Or thereabouts – it burns me and it saves me –
Or say the single one is the pakeha fish

And the big one Te Ariki
Followed by te tuna, the Maori fish

Who twists on after Him in poverty and darkness,
And I must go with them upstream to the heart of the cross.

*21*

Can this poor donkey ever carry Him
Into Hiruharama? Everything stands against it,

But that is the Rider's problem – on my kitchen shelf I keep
The square awkward tin that Agnes gave me

The day I left here going north,
A blind man walking – inside she put for me

Bread and cake and potted eel
To give me strength on that slow journey

To the mills of Hatana – now I am back here again;
The bread is gone, the eel is eaten,

And Hatana has written on the marrow of my bones
One kind of understanding – Agnes, I think, is out of it –

In Wanganui in her sister's house
Where the trees are cut down by the chainsaw and the ripsaw.

## 22

Let the Maker of rainbows and mountains do what He wishes
With this poor idiot, this crab in His beard

Who will not be dislodged – becoming, as it were,
Available is all my science,

And what He will do He will do – the problem is
Not our existence, Colin, but our arrogance

That wants to run the party – tomorrow I plant potatoes
With any luck, secretly nourishing them

With my own dung, carried with a trowel
From the giant maimai – not wishing to scandalize

Anybody – that is one job I can do
While He lets me do it; another is to pray

That He'll send me, in His good time, a tuakana
To work alongside me and instruct me in these matters.

*23*

First I strip the sods off; then I shake them
To get the earth loose, and carry them

A few yards to make a wall that might
Shelter some beans – Sister Aquinas in her

Dark blue dress hoeing beside the cowshed
Tells me – 'The couch grass seems to grow the more,

'The more you cultivate' – I lay the long white roots
Inside a broken tank for the sun to kill

By slow roasting; and begin to spade the earth,
Diagonally of course – this man has to make a game

Even out of digging; my pants and shirt
From Father Te Awhitu; my boots from the Vincent de Paul

Society – when the wind flutters round my chest
It seems to say, 'Now, now, don't be proud that you are poor!'

## 24

The kids here don't shout out, 'Jesus!'
Or, 'Hullo, Moses!' as they did in Auckland

When they saw my hair – these ones are too polite –
They call me Mr Baxter when they bring the milk;

I almost wish they didn't; but Sister has them well trained –
And soon she wants me to give them a talk about drugs;

What should I say? – 'Children, your mothers and your fathers
Get stoned on grog; in Auckland they get stoned on pot;

'It does no harm at all, as far as I know
From smoking it; but the big firms are unloading

'Pep pills for slimming, tablets for sleeping,
On the unlucky world – those ones can drive you mad –

'Money and prestige are worse drugs than morphine' –
That way I'd hit the target; but I doubt if the nuns would think it wise.

## 25

The brown river, te taniwha, flows on
Between his banks – he could even be on my side,

I suspect, if there is a side – there are still notches worn
In the cliffs downstream where they used to shove

The big canoes up; and just last week some men
Floated a ridge-pole down from an old pa

For the museum – he can also be
A brutal lover; they say he sucked under

A young girl once, and the place at the river-bend is named
After her tears – I accept that – I wait for

The taniwha in the heart to rise – when will that happen?
Is He dead or alive? A car goes by on the road

With an enormous slogan advertising
Rides for tourists on the jetboat at Pipiriki.

## 26

'Under a naked Master it does not fit well
The disciple to be too dainty' – so I paraphrase

The words of Bernard; for comfort, Colin, comfort
May kill the heart – so then, if the Dettol burns my jowls,

If the earth splits my fingers, if the wind is sharp
Blowing from banks of cloud as I go out

In a thin shirt, it is only to avoid
Being too dainty – the yogi Milarepa,

My son told me, lived for years on nettle soup
And his sister called him a fool – 'an ascetic hedonist',

Our theologians might comment – but how do they fight
The world and the flesh in their universities?

The naked Master who hangs above my door
Gave up, like old Milarepa, His bones to the bonfire.


*27*

Three dark buds for the Trinity
On one twig I found in the lining of my coat

Forgotten since I broke them from the tree
That grows opposite the RSA building

At the top of Vulcan Lane – there I would lay down my parka
On the grass and meditate, cross-legged; there was a girl

Who sat beside me there;
She would hold a blue flower at the centre of the bullring

While the twigs on the tree became black
And then slowly green again – she was young – if I had said,

'Have my coat; have my money' –
She would have gone away; but because I gave her nothing

She came again and again to share that nothing
Like a bird that nests in the open hand.

## 28

In a room full of smoke now that the stove is lit
The feeling of being on a space-ship bound for Mars

Is taking charge – the wing of the noonday demon,
I think, though he happens to visit me at night,

The hermit's familiar – What does he say? – something
Like this – 'You should be somewhere else, brother,

'Anywhere else; this stagnant life is bad,
Much too limited for a bloke of your talents

'Such as – well, you name them! – in the frame of modern life
You'd be better off doing – it doesn't matter what,

'As long as it isn't – well, digging in cow manure,
Eating, sleeping' – (he doesn't mention praying) –

'And as for that notion of yours of founding a tribe,
Hell, you're on your own here!' – I squash him like a weta
        with the shovel.


## 29

Our Lady shifted the demons; no need to talk about it;
It is her habit, lucid, warm,

Miraculous – but if you are consulted
One day, Colin, about my epitaph,

I suggest these words – 'He was too much troubled
By his own absurdity' – though I'd prefer – 'Hemi' –

And nothing else – today my new job
Is to disentangle the roots of the fourteen small

Green cabbage plants Sister Aquinas gave me
Wrapped in damp paper – one good use, man,

For the written word! – and put them in carefully
Where the beautiful loose earth is that crumbles to the blows

Of the grubber, and later give them a little water
When the sun cannot burn their delicate leaves.

*30*

If Ngati-Hiruharama turns out to be no more than
A child's dream in the night – well then,

I have a garden, a bed to lie on,
And various company – some clattering pigeons roost

At my back door, and when I meditate in the paddock
Under the apple tree two healthy dung-smeared pigs

Strike up a conversation, imagining, I think,
I am their benefactor – that should be quite enough

To keep the bowels moving and the mind thankful;
Yet when the sun rises my delusion hears him shout

Above the river fog – 'This is the hill fort
Of our God; it is called Hiruharama!

'The goat and the opossum will find a home
Among the rocks, and the river of joy will flow from it!'


*31*

Father Te Awhitu pays me a visit
Carrying a golf club; his words are clear enough

In spite of the stroke – 'Do you think, Father,
The sins of the flesh are mainly mortal?' – 'Yes' –

'It's hard in the towns' – 'Eh, the Maori can do all right;
There's no one poor in this country' –

'I spend a lot of time writing letters;
You can plant a seed, Father, but it grows by itself in the dark

'And then only if God' – 'You know,
A thought came to me; you could write a play

'About the fight down on Moutoa Island;
A Brother was killed there' – the plate on the stove is slow

To heat up and Father leaves without his coffee;
The Maori angel has put me in my place.

138

## 32

Tormenting myself with a moral inventory
While I cut the sods and lay them straight

To make a wall to shelter beans,
I think of my two illegitimate children

And how they will judge me when they come of age;
Unfit, I grant it – yet what can a man do

Who is trying to make a wall to shelter beans
But cut the sods and lay them straight;

And what can a man do who is saddled with a woman
But love her whatever way he can

Till his guts drop out? 'Now you're a Lutheran,' mutters
The voice at my earhole; but I laugh,

Remembering the women used no rubber plugs or pills
Because they wanted to have my children.

33

Here in the morning there is no Vice Squad
To keep me on my toes – I'd cross myself once,

Say the Hail Holy Queen, then shamble out
To the kitchen to talk with Morgan – 'The house is filthy,

'Mr Baxter! That's not the way
To cure anybody' – 'Well, Mr Morgan,

'This is a kind of pakeha marae;
I'm only a lodger – you can see the one drug

'They've been using is alcohol' – Strubble would say nothing
But stroll round like a wound-up Spanish bull

While the kids climbed out of bed; I think he liked the place;
It felt like home to him – but here at 9 a.m.

There's just myself, the birds and Sister Aquinas
Knocking at the door with a bowl of dwarf beans.

## 34

I read it in the Maori primer,
'Ka timata te pupuhi o te hau' –

The wind began blowing; it blew for a century
Levelling by the musket and the law

Ten thousand meeting houses – there are two of them in the pa,
Neither one used; the mice and the spiders meet there;

And the tapu mound where the heads of chiefs were burned
Will serve perhaps one day for a golf course – yet

Their children fear te taipo,
The bush demon; on that account

They keep the lights burning all night outside their houses –
What can this pakeha fog-eater do?

Nothing; nothing! Tribe of the wind,
You can have my flesh for kai, my blood to drink.


*35*

The trap I am setting to catch a tribe
Is all but furnished – on Friday Father Condon

Will (if he remembers) bring from Ohakune
The crucifix my friend Milton carved

With its garments made of wood shavings
And a faceless face, Maori or pakeha either

As the light catches it; also the workman Buddha
Hoani lent me, and the Hindu image of Mara

Trix handed on so as to be wholly poor –
What else, Colin? They say it is best

To break a rotten egg in the creek
To get eels – I think I am that egg

And Te Ariki must crack me open
If the fish are to be drawn in at all.

## 36

Brother Ass, Brother Ass, you are full of fancies,
You want this and that – a woman, a thistle,

A poem, a coffeebreak, a white bed, no crabs;
And now you complain of the weight of the Rider

Who will set you free to gallop in the light of the sun!
Ah well, kick Him off then, and see how you go

Lame-footed in the brambles; your disconsolate bray
Is ugly in my ears – long ago, long ago,

The battle was fought and the issue decided
As to who would be King – go on, little donkey

Saddled and bridled by the Master of the world,
Be glad you can distinguish not an inch of the track,

That the stones are sharp, that your hide can itch,
That His true weight is heavy on your back.


## 37

Colin, you can tell my words are crippled now;
The bright coat of art He has taken away from me

And like the snail I crushed at the church door
My song is my stupidity;

The words of a homely man I cannot speak,
Home and bed He has taken away from me;

Like an old horse turned to grass I lift my head
Biting at the blossoms of the thorn tree;

Prayer of priest or nun I cannot use,
The songs of His house He has taken away from me;

As blind men meet and touch each other's faces
So He is kind to my infirmity;

As the cross is lifted and the day goes dark
Rule over myself He has taken away from me.

## 38

'I am dying now because I do not die' –
The song of the thief who hangs upon the tree;

'The house where I was born had seven windows
But its door is closed to me;

Whether I robbed or not I have forgotten,
My death has taken hold of me;

There was a woman once who gave me a cup of wine
And her eyes were full of mercy;

There is not even judgement any more
In the place where I have to be;

I cannot turn my head to find out
Who hangs beside me on the other tree;

Let the woman who is standing down below
Say a prayer for him and me.'

## 39

In Auckland it was the twelve days' garland,
Feast with friends and shouting in the streets;

Now it is the apex and the clean flint knife –
Colin, if you meet him, give my love

To Patric Carey, and if you have the time
Once or twice go out to Brighton

To visit my parents – easy to hang
Imperatives on a good friend from a distance,

But I say, 'If' – one thing, how can the image come
At all to the centre where the mind is silent

Without being false? I had hoped for fifty sonnets,
But here are thirty-nine, my gift to you, Colin,

From Hiruharama,
From Hemi te tutua.

## The Labyrinth

*(for John Weir)*

So many corridors, – so many lurches
On the uneven filthy floor
Daedalus made and then forgot, – 'What *right*
Have you to be here?' the demons thick as roaches
Whispering . . .
          Mind fixed on the Minotaur
I plugged onward like a camel that first night,
Thinking – 'Not long, brother, not long now!' –
But now so many nights have passed
The problem is to think of him at all
And not of, say, the fact that I am lost
Or the spark of light that fell upon my brow
From some high vault, – I sit down like a little girl
To play with my dolls, – sword, wallet and the god's great amulet
My father gave me.
          In the bullfights it was easy
(Though heroic no doubt) because their eyes, their eyes held me
To the agile task. Now I am a child
Frightened by falling water, by each nerve-pricking memory
Of things ill done, – but I do not forget
One thing, the thread, the invisible silk I hold
And shall hold till I die.
          I tell you, brother,
When I throw my arms around the Minotaur
Our silence will be pure as gold.


## Winter Monologue

One has to die here on earth,
My beard has got the stink of the ground already,

The opossum thuds in the roof like a man dropping bricks,
My belly is content enough

With two cups of tea and two bits of cake
Wehe gave me today as I sat on her doorstep,

But the night comes like a hammer cracking on an anvil
And all nga mokai huddle in the big house,

Playing the guitar, lighting up the little stove,
Not finding fault – one has to die

In order to water the roots of the tree with blood,
Guts, nerves, brains – once I was a word-maker,

Now my bones are buried at Hiruharama,
But the bones talk, brother. They say – 'Winter burns us like black
    fire!'

Ah well, soon I will go up the hill
To where the drain and the ditch and the new pipe

Are tangled in the dark – How cold it is!
The plumber has laid on running water

From the spring above the road – water, water,
That has to flow in the furrows of the garden,

That has to wash dishes, pots, old muddy clothes,
That has to be added to porridge or coffee

Before we can eat or drink – water is the sign of God,
Common, indispensable, easy to overlook –

How cold it is! Death will kill the cold
With one last stab, they say, and bring us to the sun-bright fields
    of Canaan,

But I must stay outside till the last of nga mokai
Straggle in – time then to soak myself in the hot springs of
    Heaven!

## The Ikons

Hard, heavy, slow, dark,
Or so I find them, the hands of Te Whaea

Teaching me to die. Some lightness will come later
When the heart has lost its unjust hope

For special treatment. Today I go with a bucket
Over the paddocks of young grass,

So delicate like fronds of maidenhair,
Looking for mushrooms. I find twelve of them,

Most of them little, and some eaten by maggots,
But they'll do to add to the soup. It's a long time now

144

Since the great ikons fell down,
God, Mary, home, sex, poetry,

Whatever one uses as a bridge
To cross the river that only has one beach,

And even one's name is a way of saying –
'This gap inside a coat' – the darkness I call God,

The darkness I call Te Whaea, how can they translate
The blue calm evening sky that a plane tunnels through

Like a little wasp, or the bucket in my hand,
Into something else? I go on looking

For mushrooms in the field, and the fist of longing
Punches my heart, until it is too dark to see.

### Conversation in a Garden

In the garden beside the dry swimming pool
Behind the big house, I recite the Third

Joyful Mystery in the company of Anne
Who stands as high as my right tit. It is certainly

An affluent neighbourhood, and the sludge tanks of the town
Empty into the tidal river

So that whatever fish you happen to pull out
Will twist your gut with typhoid. If I took the liberty

Of pissing against the door of the local gasworks
There would be thunder. Reverberations,

Let us say. The river runs to the sea
Swollen to its bank with weeping from the hills

For what was lost in the Land Wars. Anne is uncertain
Whether to go to Varsity in Hamilton,

The land of LSD, or head back with this
Hairy etcetera to a windowless hutch

At Jerusalem. I tell her that obedience
Is pleasing to God and suitable for a woman

145

Under seventeen. Her parents have no doubt
Concerning the best course. Nor have I.

There is no river where the typhoid bug
Has not established its delicate tyranny.


### News from a Pacified Area

The day of anger after the holy night
Will bring down corpses from the broken hills

Rotating like rubber ducks. All corpses are the same.
These were villagers who preferred something

To something else, or had the lack of wisdom
Not to dig deeper than moles when men came

With gas and grenades. Death is a good master.
He pays us and does not expect us to learn

The difficult art of keeping sane. We heard
The raped girl yelling in the barn

And when their leader showed his head
It was our own troops. Her grandfather's dramatics

Were singularly useless. I have no interest
In bucking the odds. My sister who became

Different tells me you can grow fat as a hen
Scratching in the shadow of the guns. My father,

For the last time I put melons on your grave,
And promise – what? Vengeance? Hope?

To distinguish the assassin from the victim
Would take God's knowledge, and he is dead

Because he requires our love to keep him in life,
And love is not our talent. I have grown a face

Whitish and smooth, like new scar tissue, brother,
To hide the evidence I am no longer I.


146

## Morning in Jerusalem

A cloud above the range like a honeycomb
Slowly being built, is what I groove on

From the window of the smallest whare, –
While I scratch my legs for fleas

And hear the others shifting in their dreams, –
Pure and wild the cloudbank, but later

It will be red and black for rain
Sitting in drops on the round leaves

Of the vines that wrap the broken branches
On the river edge below the pa, –

Rain comes from the east, as I put on trousers
White with feathers from a bust mattress,

The same shirt as usual, and the coat
With holes in the elbows and leather cuffs

I got from the Maori Welfare Officer, –
A head full of mud, a festering foot,

Wet grassheads whipping my knees on the track to the cottage,
And this is Hiruharama, the dark

Crucible of the alchemist
Where what is not can marry what is, –

So they say, the visitors who leave me
To make bricks with blood for mortar.


## He Waiata mo Te Kare

### 1

Up here at the wharepuni
That star at the kitchen window
Mentions your name to me.

Clear and bright like running water
It glitters above the rim of the range,

You in Wellington,
I at Jerusalem,

Woman, it is my wish
Our bodies should be buried in the same grave.

## 2

To others my love is a plaited kono
Full or empty,
With chunks of riwai,
Meat that stuck to the stones.

To you my love is a pendant
Of inanga greenstone,
Too hard to bite,
Cut from a boulder underground.

You can put it in a box
Or wear it over your heart.

One day it will grow warm,
One day it will tremble like a bed of rushes
And say to you with a man's tongue,
'Taku ngakau ki a koe!'

## 3

I have seen at evening
Two ducks fly down
To a pond together.

The whirring of their wings
Reminded me of you.

## 4

At the end of our lives
Te Atua will take pity
On the two whom he divided.

To the tribe he will give
Much talking, te pia and a loaded hangi.

To you and me he will give
A whare by the seashore
Where you can look for crabs and kina
And I can watch the waves
And from time to time see your face
With no sadness,
Te Kare o Nga Wai.

5

No rafter paintings,
No grass-stalk panels,
No Maori mass,

Christ and his Mother
Are lively Italians
Leaning forward to bless,

No taniko band on her head,
No feather cloak on his shoulder,

No stairway to heaven,
No tears of the albatross.

Here at Jerusalem
After ninety years
Of bungled opportunities,
I prefer not to invite you
Into the pakeha church.

6

Waves wash on the beaches.
They leave a mark for only a minute.
Each grey hair in my beard
Is there because of a sin,

The mirror shows me
An old tuatara,
He porangi, he tutua,
Standing in his dusty coat.

I do not think you wanted
Some other man.

149

I have walked barefoot from the tail of the fish to the nose
To say these words.

7

Hilltop behind hilltop,
A mile of green pungas
In the grey afternoon
Bow their heads to the slanting spears of rain.

In the middle room of the wharepuni
Kat is playing the guitar, –
'Let it be! Let it be!'

Don brings home a goat draped round his shoulders.
Tonight we'll eat roasted liver.

One day, it is possible,
Hoani and Hilary might join me here,
Tired of the merry-go-round.

E hine, the door is open,
There's a space beside me.

*8*

Those we knew when we were young,
None of them have stayed together,
All their marriages battered down like trees
By the winds of a terrible century.

I was a gloomy drunk.
You were a troubled woman.
Nobody would have given tuppence for our chances,
Yet our love did not turn to hate.

If you could fly this way, my bird,
One day before we both die,
I think you might find a branch to rest on.

I chose to live in a different way.

Today I cut the grass from the paths
With a new sickle,
Working till my hands were blistered.

I never wanted another wife.

150

## 9

Now I see you conquer age
As the prow of a canoe beats down
The plumes of Tangaroa.

You, straight-backed, a girl,
Your dark hair on your shoulders,
Lifting up our grandchild,

How you put them to shame,
All the flouncing girls!

Your face wears the marks of age
As a warrior his moko,
Double the beauty,
A soul like the great albatross

Who only nests in mid ocean
Under the eye of Te Ra.

You have broken the back of age.
I tremble to see it.

## 10

Taraiwa has sent us up a parcel of smoked eels
With skins like fine leather.
We steam them in the colander.
He tells us the heads are not for eating,

So I cut off two heads
And throw them out to Archibald,
The old tomcat. He growls as he eats
Simply because he's timid.

Earlier today I cut thistles
Under the trees in the graveyard,
And washed my hands afterwards,
Sprinkling the sickle with water.

That's the life I lead,
Simple as a stone,
And all that makes it less than good, Te Kare,
Is that you are not beside me.

# Autumn Testament

## 1

As I come down the hill from Toro Poutini's house
My feet are sore, being bare, on the sharp stones

And that is a suitable penance. The dust of the pa road
Is cool, though, and I can see

The axe of the moon shift down behind the trees
Very slowly. The red light from the windows

Of the church has a ghostly look, and in
This place ghosts are real. The bees are humming loudly

In moonlight in their old hive above the church door
Where I go in to kneel, and come out to make my way

Uphill past a startled horse who plunges in the paddock
Above the nunnery. Now there are one or two

Of the tribe back in the big house – What would you have me do,
King Jesus? Your games with me have turned me into a boulder.

## 2

Wahi Ngaro, the void from which all life comes,
Has given us these woven spider-cages

That tie together the high heads of grass,
A civilization in each. A stick can rip the white silk,

But that is not what I will do, having learnt
With manhood mercy, if no other good,

Two thousand perhaps in the tribe of nga mokai
Scattered like seeds now in the bins and the jails

Or occupied at their various occasions
Inside the spider-cage of a common dream,

Drugs, work, money. Siân, Kat,
Don and Francie, here with me at home

In the wharepuni – One great white flower
Shakes in the wind, turning a blind head towards our veranda.

## 3

Now we are short of meat, but up the path
Don comes carrying a goat on his shoulders

And I am astonished. 'What do you know,' he asks me,
'About butchering?' 'Not a bloody thing!'

Yet tonight I read a book by Debray the revolutionary
At the table where two candles burn

In front of the crucified Hero Father Theodore gave us,
While Don plays the guitar and Kat is talking

And Francie takes a bath in the other room,
And the dinner was good – half a goat's heart, a kidney and one
    testicle,

With cabbage and soya beans. Out on the hills
The moreporks are calling with human voices,

As the pa people tell us, for someone about to die,
But that could be anybody. Tonight we have our peace.

## 4

Wahi Ngaro, the gap from which our prayers
Fall back like the toi-toi arrows

Children shoot upwards – Wahi Ngaro,
The limitless, the silent, the black night sky

From which the church huddles like a woman
On her hillock of ground – into your wide arms

Travelling, I forget the name of God,
Yet I can hear the flies roam through the rooms

Now at midday, feel the wind that flutters
The hippie goddess picture somebody painted

On an old blind and nailed on the wall. I can see
The orange flowers withering in a milk bottle,

Taste my tobacco phlegm, touch, if I like, the great bronze Christ
Theodore put up, on the poles of a cross he cut and bound
    himself.

Wahi Ngaro, now the ego like a sentry
At the gate of the soul closes its eyelids

For a moment, as today when
A crowd of ducks rose flapping at the place

Above the rapids where I go to bathe
Naked, splashing the water on my thighs,

And later I walked barefoot over the smooth boulders,
Thinking, 'There need be no other Heaven

'Than this world' – but rain spat soon
Out of a purple cloud, and I hid under

The willow leaves and bramble, as Adam did
Once from the Father. I brought back for Francie

A sprig of wet wild mint
That should go well tomorrow with the potatoes.

6

The darkness of oneself returns
Now that the house is empty,

A sense of danger in the room half dark,
Half lighted, seen through a squarish doorway,

Sticky rings left by cups on the table,
Darkness, the flutter of a moth,

A table spread in a tomb for the dead to eat at, –
That's it, the Dead! – 'Why did you pay

'A visit to Toro at night? Night is the time for the morepork,'
Wehe told me today, as we sat down to

Fried Maori bread, meat and pickle,
We who will certainly each of us one day return

To our mother the grave. The darkness of oneself
Comes from knowing nothing can be possessed.

## 7

To wake up with a back sore from the hard mattress
In a borrowed sleeping bag

Lent me by Anne – it was her way, I think,
Of giving at the same time a daughter's

And a mother's embrace – friend, daughter, mother –
These kids have heart enough to nourish the dead world

Like David in his bed – to wake up and see
The sun, if not the light from behind the sun,

Glittering on the leaves beside the graveyard
Where some of them cleared the bramble and placed on the
    bare slab

A jam jar full of flowers – to wake is to lift up
Again on one's shoulder this curious world

Whose secret cannot be known by any of us
Until we enter Te Whiro's kingdom.

*8*

Brothers, the green walnuts are swelling
On the tree below the hill,

Round and hard, the shape of a man's scrotum,
And later on they'll fall in the grass

For us and the pa people. I sit in the transport shed
This morning of autumn, with the sun shining

And not a single cloud. Ria, Toro Poutini,
Talk about their many grandchildren,

And I say, 'Where I grew up in the South Island
There was a rock my father used to fish from;

'Sometimes he'd set a net in the channel of the rock
To catch – the sea is the one thing I miss

'Here up the River.' Poutini tells me then,
'You have the sea as well if you have this river.'

## 9

Groper with throats like buckets,
Lazy swimming greenbone,

The rippling bulk of the stingray,
The mother shark and her young ones,

Quartz-eyed barracouta,
The iron legs of the kina,

The tribes of the octopus,
Fat flesh of the terakihi,

These images rise in sleep
Through the waters of my soul, –

As if I had been carried as a foetus
On the breast of Tangaroa,

And held in my heart an old hunger
To be dissolved and swallowed up by the waters.

*10*

The mossgrown haloed cross that crowns this church
Is too bleak for the mind of old Odysseus

Coming home to his table of rock, surviving and not surviving
Storms, words, axes, and the fingers of women,

Or the mind of Maui, who climbed inside the body
Of his ancestress and died there. Those who ride up river

In cars or the jetboat, see that high cross lifted
Above the low roofs of Jerusalem,

And speak of Mother Aubert and the Catholic Mission,
But when I see the sun fall and the moon rise

Over the edge of the ranges, I know what I have heard –
'The thoughts of a man's mind are many and secret'

To the grass of the graveyard or a woman's breast
We turn in our pain for absolution.

## 11

At times when I walk beside the budding figtree
Or on the round stones by the river,

I meet the face of my dead father
With one or two white bristles on his chin

The safety razor missed. When he was younger
He'd hold the cut-throat with the ivory handle

And bring it with one deft stroke down his jowl,
Leaving the smooth blue skin. 'Old man,' I say,

'Long loved by me, still loved by many,
Is there a chance your son will ever join you

'In the kingdom of the summer stars?' He leaves me
Without a word, but like a touch behind him,

Greener the bulge of fruit among the figleaves,
Hotter the bright eye of the noonday sun.

## 12

The wish to climb a ladder to the loft
Of God dies hard in us. The angels Jacob saw

Were not himself. Bramble is what grows best
Out of this man-scarred earth, and I don't chop it back

Till the fruit have ripened. Yesterday I picked one
And it was bitter in my mouth,

And all the ladder-climbing game is rubbish
Like semen tugged away for no good purpose

Between the blanket and the bed. I heard once
A priest rehearse the cause of his vocation,

'To love God, to serve man.' The ladder-rungs did not lessen
An ounce of his damnation by loneliness,

And Satan whistles to me, 'You! You again,
Old dog! Have you come to drop more dung at Jerusalem?'

## 13

That grove of pines I prayed so long among
For the first six months, have been cut down for firewood

Or to make the floorboards of houses in the suburbs
Where children get square eyes. A dollar a hundred feet

Seems too small a price to get
For those green candelabra of the Ascension

Whose flames were pollen, but now the grove is gone
I go instead barefoot on the bulldozed clay,

Thinking, 'The pines are Pharisees,
They shove their solemn tough-barked crowns to Heaven

'But nothing grows under them.' One day on that ripped hill,
If God desires it, there will be a house

With Maori rafters, and over its doorway painted these words:
'Te Wairua o Te Kare o Nga Wai.'

## 14

Soon I will go South to my nephew's wedding
To the quiet land I came from,

Where all the ancestors are underground
And my father now among them. On my mother's wall

The picture Theo Schoon once painted
Shows him as the Iron Duke

With lines around his chin and mouth
Carved by the ploughshare. So he did look

In the time when a Labour Government planted my brother
On the Hautu prison farm for five years

For walking in my father's footprint
And refusing to carry a gun. Now in my mother's house

The picture is an ikon. Father, is it easier to fight
The military machine, or the maggots of one's own heart?

## 15

The creek has to run muddy before it can run clear!
Here in this very room I have seen it happen,

The lads and the girls in chairs, some kneeling, some standing,
Some wearing headbands, one strumming the guitar,

And Father Theodore setting down an old
Packing case covered with a blanket

For the altar of his Mass. There was no wind
To burst the house door in, no tongues of fire,

But new skin under wounds, the Church becoming human,
As if religion were not the cemetery of hope

But a flowering branch – ah well, it was some time ago,
Sly is in jail under a two-year sentence,

Manu has gone back to the ward at Porirua,
And the Church can count her losses in Pharisaic peace.

## 16

Nobody can win that kind of battle,
I don't try it – for a month or two

At Macdonald Crescent it seemed we might be able
To twist the arm of the Public Works Department

And make them disgorge one old empty house,
But it came to nothing. The boys who sat for five hours in the
    Labour Bureau

And couldn't get the Benefit, went to clink as usual
For being out of work. I tried the Gandhijian tactic

Of fasting on coffee and lemon juice
For twenty-five days. It didn't ruffle one single

Bureaucratic feather! With no grots, no light, no water,
We cooked our rice and spuds on the open fireplace

And remember the words of Saint John of the Cross:
'Our bed of love is made among the lions' dens.'

159

## 17

In those times the fast had made me thin
Though today the spare tyre is back under my belt,

And I'd go down for a coffee at the Hungry Horse
At three a.m. when the drunks gather,

And the dark angel of the town
Would mutter, 'Man, there's no way out

'Of this labyrinth! I mean to grind your soul
And theirs, and spit you out like rotten cabbage' –

Then Sharon at the corner with five sailors
Ran across to me and held my hand –

'Hemi, I'm going to crack it for ten bucks
With each of them; that way I'll get fifty;

'I'll hate it' – Above the town flickered the wings
Of the blood-red dove of Armageddon.


## 18

Father Lenin, you understood the moment
When the soul is split clean, as a man with an axe

Will split four posts from one log of dry timber,
But then your muzhiks still had souls

That smelt the holy bread upon the altar
And knew their mother's name. The mask of money

Hides too well the wound we cannot touch,
And guns are no use to a boy with a needle

Whose world is a shrinking dome of glass
A drug from Hong Kong will splinter open

With a charging elephant on a yellow packet
For riding home to deep sleep. The dollar is the point of it,

Old Father Lenin, and your bones in the Red Square
Are clothed in roubles till the Resurrection.

## 19

The bodies of the young are not the flower,
As some may imagine – it is the soul

Struggling in an iron net of terror
To become itself, to learn to love well,

To nourish the Other – when Mumma came from the bin
With scars from the wrist to the shoulder,

They combed her hair and put their arms around her
Till she began to blossom. The bread she baked for us

Was better kai than you'd get in a restaurant
Because her soul was in it. The bread we share in the churches

Contains a Christ nailed up in solitude,
And all our pain is to be crystal vases,

As if the mice were afraid of God the cat
Who'd plunge them into Hell for touching one another.

## 20

Somebody in my dream was shaking a blanket
Sending a gust of wind with dust and fleas

Over my body – and when I woke,
In the dark room I saw a wavering shape

Like a vampire in a castle in the stories
I used to read as a boy. Whether or not it came

From the graveyard forty feet away
From the house corner, fear increases the strength

Of any kehua – so I crossed over and switched on the light,
Smoked a cigarette, chewed over a few pages

Of Peter Marin, and began to write this poem,
Since a man who'll die some day should hardly fear the dead,

And the tribe need a father who is afraid only
Of ceasing to love them well.

## 21

King Jesus, after a day or a week of bitching
I come back always to your bread and salt,

Because no other man, no other God,
Suffered our pains with us minute by minute

And asked us to die with him. Not even guilty,
This morning I say the *Salve Regina*

While the fog is shifting slowly out of the trees,
Fry four slices of bread and eat them,

Then sit down under the image that stood once
In a Dutch farmhouse, then in a room in Putaruru,

Now in this place. It is perhaps the nimbus
Of Theodore's thick body and solar heart

That clings to the bronze, bringing to mind
Abundant loaves and multiplying fishes.


*22*

To pray for an easy heart is no prayer at all
Because the heart itself is the creaking bridge

On which we cross these Himalayan gorges
From bluff to bluff. To sweat out the soul's blood

Midnight after midnight is the ministry of Jacob,
And Jacob will be healed. This body that shivers

In the foggy cold, tasting the sour fat,
Was made to hang like a sack on its thief's cross,

Counting it better than bread to say the words of Christ,
'*Eli! Eli!*' The Church will be shaken like a

Blanket in the wind, and we are the fleas that fall
To the ground for the dirt to cover. Brother thief,

You who are lodged in my ribcage, do not rail at
The only gate we have to paradise.

## 23

The heat moves into my bones again
Here on the edge of the veranda

Father Te Awhitu mended hour by hour
With new boards where the rain had rotted them

Pouring down from a roof that has no spouting,
And when I asked him why, replied, 'Mahi mo Te Atua' –

'Work done for God' – the day the house was ready
I lit the stove in the front room,

That cost me twenty dollars secondhand in Wanganui
And had a broken lid – wood, stove, matches,

The first flame rising – so the house became
Inhabited with the flame of non-possession

That burns now and always in the heart of the tribe,
Too simple a thing for the world to understand.

## 24

The brown grass that Barry cut for us
With the new sickle, is lying in heaps

Between the house and the door of the pataka
Where we stuck our mattresses. Barry has gone

Perhaps to Oakley where they'll pump him full of drugs
And ask him the meaning of the tattoos on his arm

'Dad; Love; Hate' – he used to sail like a swan
Through the middle of the Courtroom up to the dock,

His coat split above the buttocks,
Boots loud on the floor, his forelock hanging

Over one eye, then tossed back, a débutante
Under the gaze of his friends. The fuzz were

Ignorant lovers in that brain-smashing courtship
Where love words are swearwords and kisses are blows.

## 25

Richard will not come here, the shy one,
Wary as a crayfish whose feelers jut out

From a crevice in the rock. When he was thirteen,
In the maths class, his teacher used to stand him

In a wastepaper basket at the front of the room,
And once I heard the lawyer ask him,

'Can't you think of something better to do with your life?'
'No.' The face like a young stone mask:

'Idiots have no opinions.'
I heard him breaking bottles in the street

The night Naomi turned him down;
Naomi was a mother who had found him

Too hard to carry. Yet he broke no windows.
It hurts me to watch the snaring of the unicorn.

I go up the road under the eye of Te Ra,
And a cicada flying gets tangled in my hair

Until I set him free. Just as I finish
The Mystery of the Crowning with Thorns,

Rex pulls up in his truck – 'The new overseer
Is a little Hitler . . . The gristle's gone from my hipbone,

'When I lie down in bed the bones pull
Out of their socket.' He drives on through the dust.

I keep him in mind through the Carrying of the Cross,
Then kneel for God's Death by the black plastic tank

Where troughs are stuck in the moss to catch
The meagre trickle of midsummer

That flows through the pipe to the house. It's cool up here
Under the green ribbed branches of the pungas.

When I stayed those three months at Macdonald Crescent
In the house of Lazarus, three tribes were living

In each of the storeys – on the ground floor, the drunks
Who came there when the White Lodge burnt down;

Above them, the boobheads; and scattered between the first
And second storey, the students who hoped to crack

The rock of education. The drunks are my own tribe.
One Sunday, the pubs being shut, they held a parliament

In the big front room – Lofty with his walking stick,
Phil the weeper, Taffy who never spoke much,

And one or two others – in conclave they sat, like granite columns
Their necks, like Tritons their faces,

Like tree-roots their bodies. Sober as Rhadamanthus
They judged the town and found it had already been judged.

## 28

Both the girls are sick. I find it a drag
To cook kai for the two of them,

Ferry cups of tea, read some verse to Francie,
Or carry a blanket for Siân – that's honest enough!

I do it. It has its moments.
I meant to go and rave down at Otaki

Among the Catholic laymen, but this is more to the point
With Kat and Don away. Francie becomes active,

Sleeps in draughts, wanders through the house,
Siân lies quiet in a Buddhist cloud

Of 'flu bugs and vegetarian torpor,
A girl from the Welsh hills. The mood of family

Soon takes over, and they become my daughters,
I their Granpop. We get to know each other well.

## 29

I think the Lord on his axe-chopped cross
Is laughing as usual at my poems,

My solemn metaphors, my ladder-climbing dreams,
For he himself is incurably domestic,

A family man who never lifted a sword,
An only son with a difficult mother,

If you understand my thought. He has saddled me again
With the cares of a household, and no doubt

Has kept me away from Otaki
Because I'd spout nonsense, and wear my poverty

As a coat of vanity. Down at the Mass
Today, as Francie told me to, I took Communion

For her (and Siân as well) cursing gently
The Joker who won't let me shuffle my own pack.

## 30

Simply for bowing one's head in a little matter,
Strange that so great a peace should come!

I find that the flower like a star beside the power pole
Is made up of thirty separate flower-heads,

Each one a different blossom – why, I can't say,
But the light of God shines out of them,

The delicate pure invisible light I have not
Seen since I left Grafton. In those days

I'd climb the hill on the Domain
Before dawn, when the leaves were cold as iron

Underfoot, and talk with the trees – this one
Thinking she was ugly in her narrow dress of bark,

That one a woman who'd had many children –
The tree nymphs – their great beauty made me tremble.

## 31

I tell the girls, 'After long meditation,
Scrutiny of books in Arabic and Latin,

'Consultation (by telephone) with twenty-five colleagues,
Examination with bioscope and xylophone,

'I have come to the crux of my diagnosis,
Your ailment is a hybrid,

'Tuberculosis, cholera, leprosy,
In one package' – they are not impressed,

Nor, I think, is the master of the house,
The Maori sergeant from the First World War

In uniform, seated on a cane chair
In the foot-high photograph upon our mantelpiece.

I think he has summed us up – 'Kaore nga pukapuka!
You might stay well if you learnt Maoritanga.'


## 32

Life can be a hassle. Are you free of it, Monsignor,
While you dispute the changes of the liturgy

Or polish up your golf style? At one p.m.
Either in your house or my house

The soul may plunge into pain like a child who slides
Through the grass at the lip of a mine-shaft,

Therefore don't ask me, 'What do you mean by that statement
You made to the *Weekly News*?' – or – 'What precisely is

'Your relation to Sally X – ?' A man is a bubble
Sticking to the edge of a mighty big drainpipe!

Let us be content to play one game of chess,
Share a coffee and biscuit, let Christ work out the deficit, –

There were eight souls, they say, with Father Noah;
Neither you nor I might have made it to the gangplank.

## 33

'Mother, your statue by the convent path
Has chips of plaster scattered round it

'Where rain or frost have stripped you of your mantle – '
'It doesn't matter.' 'As you know, in winter

'I often kneel there under the knife-edged moon
Praying for – ' 'I hear those prayers.'

'Mother, your blue gown seems like stone,
Too rigid – ' 'What they make of me

'Is never what I am.' 'Our Church looks to the young
Like a Medusa; they want to be – '

'Free, yes; Christ is the only Master.'
'They are taught to judge themselves.' 'Suffer it.'

'But sin – ' 'I see no sin. My secret is
I hold the Child I was given to hold.'

## 34

At evening the sandflies would rise from the river
And bite our bare ankles where we waited

For a tug on the line. Peter had dug
A pit in the bank to throw the eels in,

And when we caught one he tossed it there
To twist like a snake, the slime on its body

Plastered with mud. 'Hemi, pray for a catch.'
'It's quiet on the water;

'God is here.' We caught two more,
And took the first one up to Koro Rangi

In case he wanted a kai. One eel fed twelve people,
But Peter was a chef. Carl put five eels in the bath

And studied them with an elf's attention,
The way their fins moved, the way they intertwined.

## 35

The stove will blaze here in the winter
Heating the whole room. We still need

Blankets, money for kai, money for lighting,
Stones laid on the path between the house and the cottage,

New iron and paint for the roof, some window glass,
Five or six chairs, two doors, a fridge for the meat,

A veranda beam and spouting – Good to be poor!
Without God our boat will sink,

And that is the way it should be. The blind man hoisted
The lame man on his back, and then the blind man

Had eyes, the lame man, legs. By his old habit,
I'd say, God will let us wait till the boat is sinking

Then bail it out in a minute. Still that man goes
Walking on the water and thinking his own thoughts.

## 36

This fine windy morning I think about
The leper lying beside the fruitstalls in Calcutta

Under the shade of the great bridge. The oil-stained bandages
Around his limbs, the flies moving slowly

In and out of his nostrils, over his eyelids;
That lion face of dark mahogany

Turned up its brow to the overlying cloud
Behind which Rahm might live, from which a few spots

Of rain aspersed the pavement. I threw some coins
Into his tin dish. The policeman, built like a Maori

Guarding the fruitstalls in his khaki shorts,
Said, 'They're no use to him.' But the man was not quite dead.

When he was younger he should have had a gun.
There or in Karori, the sickness is, not to be wanted.

## 37

I have seen them play the guitar round the bonfire
Out there on the grass, night after night,

With a little beer and a few roasted potatoes,
But now the tribe has gone. Ella, Warwick,

Abe, Red Steve, Moth, Belligerent Mike,
And fifty others – when I meet them on the pavements

Their heads hang down, the mask is back again
By which the town holds itself together,

But here they needed no mask. Abe, with one lung
Deflated, would wheeze all night like a blowhole

Behind a curtain in the top bunk,
But I saw him with a shovel in the bottom of the pit

They dug for the shithouse, tossing earth to the sky,
His dark face wrinkled with the tribal smile.

Last night a grey nimbus round the moon,
Today the rain comes from the west;

The leaves on all the trees look greener,
Rangimotu is burning piles of dry grass in his garden,

The flames go up to the low heaven,
And Wehe shouts to him from the door of her kitchen,

'You, come in out of the rain!' He only smiles
And goes on raking. I carry up the hill

A milk bottle full of sauce, bread and a parcel of sausages;
I plug the jug in and wait for it to boil

While the girls lie in bed. 'I like the rain.'
'I like it too. Aren't you afraid, Hemi,

'Of catching the 'flu?' 'Not exactly.
It's only that – ' The rain comes down in a dense white curtain.

The centre of our dreaming is the cave
That the world translates as brothel. Margaret told me once

A dream she had, about a house
In a meadow by the sea, old and full of passages,

Upstair and downstair rooms where the tribe were sleeping,
And three great waves came out of the sea

And washed around the house and left it standing,
Though for a while they had hidden the sun and the moon.

There has to be, I think, some shelter,
A home, an all-but-God, an all-but-mother

In time and place, not just the abstract void
Of I looking for me. Around these walls

They dipped their hands in paint and left their handprints
As on the walls of caves the Magdalenian hunters.

40

Three tourists come out of the church and stand on the grass rim
Above the pa. One of them points

At the big hall roofed with new iron
And walled with plaster board, where the men who built the
    bridge

Cooked their meals and slept at night
'That's where the hippies lived. They had to kick them out.'

'They couldn't do much harm in this place.'
Their eyes are lenses looking at the houses,

Five or six, two of them windowless,
And missing out the aroha. Their fantasies will never

Be shifted in a world that's built to turn
On Us and Them. An old fear grips my belly

When I hear the brassed-off voices of the executioners
Who may one day come to burn us out of our burrow.

## 41

Twenty buckets of water for the bath,
And then another seven or so

Because it's too hot. 'Thank you, Hemi,'
Francie lisps in the small-child voice

She uses as one mask among a dozen,
But that is her privilege. She has not yet got over

The fire-walking ceremony of the Plymouth Brethren
And maybe never will. We each have

Our necessary games. But at this house
Where all things hang from moss-bearded branches

The hernias of the mind retract themselves
Month by month. The ones who used to come here

Like divers to a decompression chamber
Staggering, won't come again. I have to say, 'So be it.'

## 42

The rata blooms explode, the bow-legged tomcat
Follows me up the track, nipping at my ankle,

The clematis spreads her trumpet, the grassheads rattle
Ripely, drily, and all this

In fidelity to death. Today when Father Te Awhitu
Put on the black gown with the silver cross,

It was the same story. The hard rind of the ego
Won't ever crack except to the teeth of Te Whiro,

That thin man who'll eat the stars. I can't say
It pleases me. In the corner I can hear now

The high whining of a mason fly
Who carries the spiders home to his house

As refrigerated meat. 'You bugger off,' he tells me,
'Your Christianity won't put an end to death.'

## 43

On the willows Don has felled by Poutini's cottage
The leaves are heavy with reddish galls,

Lumps like oval cysts, and if you break them open
You find inside a pale thin grub

Arching its body. When I came up from the town
My feet had spreading lumps that filled with fluid,

Hard as an egg and larger than a finger,
Got by walking on the roasting asphalt

Below Macdonald Crescent. The life of the streets dug in,
Taking charge. I thought my feet were rotting.

Keri brought me some strips of bark his father
Had cut in the hills. I boiled the bark for half an hour,

Poured that water into a plastic tub
And soaked my feet. In two days the lumps were gone.

## 44

This testament, a thing of rags and patches,
Will end soon. I cannot say, like Villon,

'Pray for me and for yourselves,'
For this is another century. That poor man ate his lunch

With the corpses of streetboys hanging overhead
And was part owner of some kind of brothel,

But the harps and lutes of paradise on the church wall
Were just as real as the bogs of fire,

The burghers sweated in their high fur gowns,
The slaves lay down to sleep on a straw mattress,

And most of it made sense. As if God had opened
A crack in the rock of the world to let some daylight in,

Saying, 'Be poor like Me.' Our life is the one
We make in darkness for ourselves.

## 45

Tomorrow I'll go down to Wellington,
Hitching, if I'm lucky, a ride down the river road

Past the karaka trees and the town houses
That turn the river into the Wanganui ditch

With shit that floats upstream below the bridges
When the tide pushes home. I'll go then

Southward among the sad green farms
Where the sheep get more freedom than their masters,

Past beaches with the plumes of toi-toi blowing
In a wind that only Maori kids on horses

Can bargain with, down, down the straight coast road
To the dream city, the old fat sow

Who smothers her children. I'll wear no diving suit
And sit cross-legged in a pub doorway.


## 46

After writing for an hour in the presbytery
I visit the church, that dark loft of God,

And make my way uphill. The grass is soaking my trousers,
The night dark, the rain falling out of the night,

And the old fears walk side by side with me,
Either the heavy thump of an apple

Hitting the ground, or the creaking of the trees,
Or the presence of two graveyards,

The new one at the house, the old one on the hill
That I have never entered. Heaven is light

And Hell is darkness, so the Christmen say,
But this dark is the belly of the whale

In which I, Jonah, have to make my journey
Till the fear has gone. Fear is the only enemy.

## 47

On the scrim of the walls the tribe have written up –
'You're all freaks' – 'Men only' –

'Humpers Unite' – 'Blessed are the peacemakers' –
'The slowest beasts are strongest and live the longest' –

'This is the tumour on Jo's brain' –
'Fuck War' – 'The Mighty Merkin' –

'Love is like nothing else but love' –
'A simple, goodly person called Mumma lived here' –

The chorus of their chaos becomes a possible Christ
When the light behind the face begins to shine,

Who wear no shoes in the street because
Rain was invented to kiss the feet of the poor.

I go south tomorrow with the river
And leave no lock on my door.

*48*

The spider crouching on the ledge above the sink
Resembles the tantric goddess,

At least as the Stone Age people saw her
And carved her on their dolmens. Therefore I don't kill her,

Though indeed there is a simpler reason,
Because she is small. Kehua, vampire, eight-eyed watcher

At the gate of the dead, little Arachne, I love you,
Though you hang your cobwebs up like dirty silk in the hall

And scuttle under the mattress. Remember I spared your children
In their cage of white cloth you made as an aerial castle,

And you yourself, today, on the window ledge.
Fear is the only enemy. Therefore when I die,

And you wait for my soul, you hefty as a king crab
At the door of the underworld, let me pass in peace.

## Te Whiore o te Kuri

### 1

Two trucks pass me in a cloud of dust
As I come up the road from the river,

So I put the bathing towel over my mouth
And breathe damp cloth. Taraiwa on the old bridge

Is cutting the iron struts with a blow torch,
But he tells me – 'Kua mutu' – 'The oxygen is finished.'

I climb the long track to the wharepuni,
Meditating on the words of Thomas Merton –

'At the end of life God presses down a seal
On the wax of the soul. If the wax is warm

'It receives the mark; if not, it is crushed to powder' –
So be it. My own heart may yet be my coffin.

Up here they give me a cup of crushed apple pulp
To drink. In autumn the kai falls from the trees.

### 2

The dark light shines from the graves of the saints,
By which I mean the humble ones

Buried beside our house and under the bramble
That hides the fallen pas where sheep are grazing

And leave their clots of wool. The dark light shines
At the heart of the tangi where a tent has been put up

To hold the coffin, and a widow with a
Three-day-sleepless face is waiting for the

Resurrection. I remember
When the church was shut at Ngaruawahia,

Kneeling instead in front of the stone statue
Of Te Whaea, darkened by rain, eroded by moss,

Under an apple tree. The dark light shines
Wherever the humble have opened a door for it.

176

### 3

A giant weta climbs the curling ladder
Of the scrim beside my bed. I don't want

The scratching of this amateur bush demon
Interfering with my dreams,

Or love-bites on my neck. First Steve comes through
With a saw – 'To cut him in half,' he says —

Then Zema – 'You're piss-poor, Hemi,
At killing' (she giggles) – but I get a shoe

From the other room, stand on the strongest chair,
Wield it by the toe and belt him – crack!

The weta, trailing white guts, drops to the floor,
A three-inch dragon in his broken armour,

Poor creature! I finish him off with another blow
And lie back to read while the mosquitoes play their flutes.

### 4

The rain falls all day. Now the tanks will be full.
The road down river will turn to wet porridge

And the slips begin. Herewini told me
How Te Atua warned him that the bank would fall,

So he left the grader and came to shift his mates, –
They ran to safety and the bank did fall

Silently, eighty tons of earth and boulders,
Burying him to the armpits. His leg is still blue

Where the great stone cracked it and the bolts were put through
    the bone,
But he can walk on it. The drips from the holes in the roof

Spatter in the kitchen, on the boards behind the stove,
At the foot of Francie's bed. Beyond the lid of cloud

I hear the droning of the birds of Armageddon
That one day will end the world we understand.

## 5

The tribe in their own time are making a fowl run
Below the big chestnut. Therefore I wake

To hear the screech of nails being dragged with hammers
At the front of the house – Steve and Gregg

Doing what once would hardly happen
In two years. One by one the girls

Come in to visit their old hairy koro
On the broad of his back in a sleeping bag

Resting his rheumatism – Te Huinga,
Zema, Francie, Cam, they bring in coffee,

But stay to sit and open out their thoughts
And put their heads on my pillow. Some people think

I keep a harem. No; my back's not strong enough.
I keep a chook pen for birds of paradise.


## 6

'Te whiore o te kuri' – this is the tail of the dog
That wags at the end of my book;

After a dispute with one dear Maori friend
I walk all night on the road to Raetihi,

Thinking, 'Twenty-four miles will pulp the pads of my feet
Till the soles of them swell up like balloons;

'Pain in my feet; pain of my hara.' This morning
I saw the sun rise molten and red

Over the hill at Herewini's house
At Raetihi. But staggering on the stones

Last night, I had to stop, and looked up at the stars
And saw those ribs of white fire

Hung there like the underside of punga leaves
Planted for our human shelter.

## 7

To go forward like a man in the dark
Is the meaning of this dark vocation;

So simple, tree, star, the bare cup of the hills,
The lifelong grave of waiting

As indeed it has to be. To ask for Jacob's ladder
Would be to mistake oneself and the dark Master,

Yet at times the road comes down to a place
Where water runs and horses gallop

Behind a hedge. There it is possible to sit,
Light a cigarette, and rub

Your bruised heels on the cold grass. Always because
A man's body is a meeting house,

Ribs, arms, for the tribe to gather under,
And the heart must be their spring of water.

## Five Sestinas

### I Winter in Jerusalem

The *I Ching* tells me *T'ai*, the sign of peace,
Is what I venture in. The pungas on the hill,
So lately loaded with snow, are green again
Though some branches were broken. Where many men gather
From need or friendship, truth begins to waken
As eels rise in the dark river.

If Heaven gives me this old house by a river,
It is not for myself, but for the purpose of peace,
As the thunder and rain of spring make green things waken,
A fence of poplar leaves between us and the hill
Who is our mother, or the chestnuts we gather
In autumn when the earth is warm again.

In our dreams it may happen the dead return again,
As if the earth spoke to us, because time is a river
On whose bank in ignorance the tribes gather

With emblems of battle, yet desiring peace.
The fathers instruct us from their holy hill
So that the warrior souls may waken.

In winter with a heavy mind I waken
And wait for the sun to lift the fogs again
That bind Jerusalem. Like a bridegroom above the hill
He touches with hands of fire the waves of the river
Like the body of a woman. Our words are words of peace
In this house where the wounded children gather.

We can go out with Maori kits to gather
Watercress, or some tough lads who waken
Early will break the veil of peace
With gunshots, combing the bush again
For young goats, or lift the eel-trap from the river
As fog shifts from the highest hill.

The times are like some rough and roadless hill
We have to climb. I do not hope to gather
Pears in winter, or halt the flow of the river
That buries in sludge the souls who begin to waken
And know themselves. Our peace can't patch again
The canoe that is broken, yet all men value peace.

Peace is the language of the pungas on the hill
Not growing for any gain. These images I gather
As eels waken in the darkness of the river.


## 2 On the Shortest Day of the Year

If the black tree ferns teach me of winter
I remember this is the house of sleep.
At morning my friends do not rouse early
And I walk by the wharepuni in the sun
With a rubber-ferruled stick and sandals on my feet,
Not worrying too much about the price of living.

They say on the marae, 'The living to the living;
The dead to the dead' – These black bones of winter
Will rise and walk with lightning in their feet
One day, but not yet. To welcome the doom of sleep
Is Adam's fate, though the molten gaze of the sun
Rouses to simple joy the birds that wake early

As if in paradise. I had to learn early
How to bear the yoke that rests on the back of the living,
The grief of all who travel beneath the sun,
Because the soul cannot cast off winter
Until Christ comes to wake her from her sleep
And the stars begin to journey on joyful feet,

Those archers with their arrows, whose proud feet
Trample above our roofs. Walking early
On the road from Raetihi, able to long for sleep,
Able to suffer pain, my body cold, but living,
A man in the grip of the dark, I saw the stars of winter
Blaze with the light but not the heat of the sun,

Rivers of fire above me. Then I craved for the sun
To shine on my wet head, to warm my feet,
To bring me alive out of the ditch of winter
Like God's arms. Here, though, I lie down early,
Comforted by the faces of the living,
Under a dry blanket, to talk and then to sleep.

If the guitar twangs till dawn, and one can't sleep,
Friends are the cause of it. Only when the sun
Lifts the valley fog do I rouse to join the living,
Drink some coffee, put sandals on my feet,
And go to walk on the grass of the marae early
Where pools of muddy water lie in winter.

I praise your winter, Lord, from the kingdom of sleep.
You shine like the early light of the sun
On a road that is hard for my feet. To be is hard for the living.


### 3 The Dark Welcome

In the rains of winter the pa children
Go in gumboots on the wet grass. Two fantails clamber
On stems of bramble and flutter their wings
In front of me, indicating a visit
Or else a death. Below the wet marae
They wait in a transport shelter for the truck to come,

Bringing tobacco, pumpkins, salt. The kai will be welcome
To my hungry wandering children
Who drink at the springs of the marae

181

And find a Maori ladder to clamber
Up to the light. The cops rarely visit,
Only the fantails flutter their wings

Telling us about the dark angel's wings
Over a house to the north where a man has come
Back from Wellington, to make a quiet visit,
Brother to one of the local children,
Because the boss's scaffolding was too weak to clamber
Up and down, or else he dreamt of the marae

When the car was hitting a bend. Back to the marae
He comes, and the fantails flutter their wings,
And the children at the tangi will shout and clamber
Over trestles, with a noise of welcome,
And tears around the coffin for one of the grown-up children
Who comes to his mother's house on a visit,

Their town cousin, making a longer visit,
To join the old ones on the edge of the marae
Whose arms are bent to cradle their children
Even in death, as the pukeko's wings
Cover her young. The dark song of welcome
Will rise in the meeting house, like a tree where birds clamber,

Or the Jacob's-ladder where angels clamber
Up and down. Thus the dead can visit
The dreams and words of the living, and easily come
Back to shape the deeds of the marae,
Though rain falls to wet the fantail's wings
As if the earth were weeping for her children.

Into the same canoe my children clamber
From the wings of the iron hawk and the Vice Squad's visit
On the knees of the marae to wait for what may come.


*4 Song to the Father*

Father, beyond the hills and water,
Beyond the city of the stars,
In a chosen overcoat of night
You hide from me. All men find it so,
And I would be a fool to grieve
Because my bones can not yet rise

Into your heaven. Now at moonrise
The glitter on the river water
Makes every stone and plant cell grieve
For what you lock behind the stars,
Promising that it will be so
But not in the now of night.

Father, I am myself the night
In whom your sun will have to rise
When death demands it must be so.
My heart dissolves in me like water
And the blunt arrows of the stars
Lodged in my marrow make me grieve.

Though it is folly still to grieve
Like a girl weeping in the night
For some king among the film stars
As if the sun could never rise
And the face of earth and water
Make true what must be so,

Father, you know that it is so,
That your kind prison makes me grieve,
The hinge of sky, the gate of water,
The floor of earth, the roof of night,
And those great warders when they rise,
The man-killing moon and stars.

Language is not enough. Your stars
Tell me because you tell them so
These bones must die before they rise,
And that is half of why I grieve.
The other half is said by the night
With tongues of air and tongues of water.

The water drowns your guardian stars
And the night wills it should be so.
This grief is only till sunrise.


## 5 *Letter to Peter Olds* [2]

The hens cackle in our kitchen
This grey day. Three of my friends
Have gone by car on the road
To Pipiriki, where the river

Takes a bend. Somebody
Is sawing wood on the grass outside

The pataka. But here, inside,
With a rooster shitting in my kitchen
I comfort an ageing body
With tobacco and words. No friends
Ever come up the river
Simply because they like the road

Or my hairy face. I think the road
To Jerusalem leads back inside
The belly of mountain and river,
As it were, to a mother's kitchen
Where all creatures are friends
Because they come from the earth's body

And God's whim. To have a body
Means to get cold feet on a road,
To need a kai, to need friends,
To patch the worn jeans on your backside,
To clean a muddy kitchen,
To drag an eel from the river,

And one or two clasp the river
In the shape of another body
Alive in the thieves' kitchen
Of earth and air. Too simple a road
For many to take it, and get outside
The hang-up of having no friends

Except for the telly. So many friends
Are drowning in the river
That flows from the wounded side
Of the doom-racked body
Of industrial man. To take this road
Back to our mother's kitchen,

Is wise, if the kitchen makes some strangers friends
In this house on a road by a river,
A tree's body with the sap inside.

## Sestina of the River Road

I want to go up the river road
Even by starlight or moonlight
Or no light at all, past the Parakino bridge,
Past Atene where the tarseal ends,
Past Koroniti where cattle run in a paddock,
Past Operiki, the pa that was never taken,

Past Matahiwi, Ranana, till the last step is taken
And I can lie down at the end of the road
Like an old horse in his own paddock
Among the tribe of Te Hau. Then my heart will be light
To be in the place where the hard road ends
And my soul can walk the rainbow bridge

That binds earth to sky. In his cave below the bridge,
Where big eels can be taken
With the hinaki, and the ends
Of willow branches trail from the edge of the road
Onto the water, the dark one rises to the light,
The taniwha who guards the tribal paddock

And saves men from drowning. Down to Poutini's paddock
The goats come in winter, and trucks cross the bridge
In the glitter of evening light
Loaded with coils of wire, five dogs, and wood
        they have taken
From a rotten fence. On the bank above the road
At the marae my journey ends

Among the Maori houses. Indeed when my life ends
I hope they find room in the paddock
Beside the meeting house, to put my bones on a road
That goes to the Maori dead. A gap I cannot bridge,
Here in the town, like a makutu has taken
Strength from my body and robbed my soul of light,

Because this blind porangi gets his light
From Hiruharama. The darkness never ends
In Pharaoh's kingdom. God, since you have taken
Man's flesh, grant me a hut in the Maori paddock
To end my life in, with their kindness as my bridge,
Those friends who took me in from the road

185

Long ago. Their tears are the road of light
I need to bridge your darkness when the world ends.
To the paddock of Te Whiti let this man be taken.


## In Times of Trouble among Nations

Through the porch window I watch the birds tumble
In a tree of yellow flowering mimosa

As the sun goes down in the pale spring sky
And the mobiles made by my friend Jane

Tinkle above my head. They are made like birds and suns
Out of some local clay

Moulded with the fingers. I remember how the Yogi
In the Tibetan village would sit in the graveyard

Juggling skulls and thigh bones, with a rope
Of entrails round his neck,

Because one has to understand
Whatever is. The sun goes down

And leaves a gap of darkness
Too fiery and cold for any man to live in.

The culture does not love its demons,
That at least is apparent – shootings, bombs, car crashes,

Or even the drip-fed drug of money
That keeps the patient quiet in his high blue bed –

But without our demons how could we exist?
We would have to look at the void!

Rasputin said, 'I learn from Mother Earth.'
He spent a month howling in a cellar,

Then told the Tsar, 'Don't send the peasants into war!
They have too much to suffer,

'The generals will get fat on stolen money,
There may be a Republic.'

Rasputin died. The tumbling birds have gone
From the mimosa. The branches look like black iron.

# Glossary of Maori Words and Phrases*

a *and*
Te Ariki *the Lord*
aroha *love*
Te Atua *God*

E *O; oh*

hangi *earth oven, or, by common usage, a feast*
Hatana *Satan*
hau *wind*
he *a; some*
Hemi *James*
hinaki *eel-trap*
hine *young woman*
Hine-nui-te-po *Goddess of Death*
Hiruharama *Jerusalem*
Hoani *John*

ihi *power*
inanga *whitebait; also a variety of greenstone*

ka *inceptive verbal particle*
kahawai *species of fish*
kai *food*
kaore *no; not*
karaka *tree with orange-yellow berries*
Te Kare *an object of affection (Baxter's name for his wife)*
Te Kare o Nga Wai *Te Kare of the waters*
kauri *massive cone-bearing forest tree prized for its timber*
kea *mountain parrot*
kehua *ghost*
ki *to*
kina *sea egg*
koe *you*
kono *woven food basket*
koro *old man (a term of respect)*
kua *particle indicating past tense*
kumara *sweet potato*
kuri *dog*

mahi *work*
maimai *hide used by duckshooters*
mako *shark*
makutu *spell; curse*
manuka *shrub or tree with aromatic leaves, often growing in dense clumps*
marae *tribal meeting-ground*
matai *species of forest tree*
Maui *mythological Maori hero, one of whose exploits was to try to kill the Death Goddess by entering her body.*

mo *for*

---

* Phrases beginning with the introductory words E, he, ka, ko, kua, nga and te are listed under the second word of the phrase.
Proper names without an English equivalent are not included.

188

moa *giant wingless bird, now extinct*
nga mokai *captives, a term also applied to the youngest members of a family. Baxter uses it to mean 'the fatherless ones'.*
moko *facial tattoo*
mutu *finished; completed*

nga *the (plural)*
ngaio *small tree found in coastal regions*
ngakau *thoughts; heart (i.e. emotions)*
Ngati Hiruharama *the Jerusalem tribe (probably refers to the members of Baxter's commune)*
nikau *palm tree*

o *of*

pa *Maori village (originally fortified)*
pakeha *New Zealander of European descent*
paraoa *bread*
pataka *store-house for food*
paua *rock shellfish*
pia *beer*
porangi *mad; madman*
puha *sowthistle (used as a vegetable)*
pukapuka *book*
pukeko *swamp-hen*
punga *tree-fern*
pupuhi *to blow, blowing*

Te Ra *the sun (by extension, God)*
rata *vine or tree with a brilliant red flower*
Te Rauparaha *nineteenth-century warrior chief of Ngati Toa*
raupo *bulrush*
rimu *forest tree prized for its timber*
riwai *potato*

taipo *devil*
taku *my*
taku ngakau ki a koe *I give my heart to you*
tama *boy; son*
Te Tama *God the Son*
Tangaroa *God of the sea*
tangi *Maori funeral ceremony; to cry*
taniko *woven band or belt*
taniwha *mythical beast inhabiting waterways and lakes*
tapu *sacred; forbidden*
te *the (singular)*
tena koe *greeting*
terakihi *species of fish*
timata *to begin*
ka timata te pupuhi o te hau *the wind began blowing*
toi-toi *tall tussocky grass with whitish-yellow plumes*
totara *large forest tree prized for its timber*
tuakana *elder brother*
tuatara *reptile resembling a large lizard*
tutua *slave; nobody*

Wahi Ngaro *the Void; Space (a term used in Maori creation chants)*
wai *water; who*
waiata *song*
He Waiata mo Te Kare *Song for Te Kare*

Te Wairua o Te Kare o Nga Wai *the spirit of Te Kare of the waters*
wairua *spirit; soul*
weta *bush insect*
Te Whaea *the Source; by extension the Mother of God*
whare *house*
whare kehua *haunted house*
wharepuni *meeting-house*
whiore *tail*
Te whiore o te kuri *the tail of the dog*
Te Whiro *Death*
Te Whiti *religious prophet and leader of the Te Ati Awa tribe who advocated a policy of passive resistance to the confiscation of Taranaki lands by the Europeans. The community he established at Parihaka was destroyed by British troops in 1881.*

# Index of Titles and First Lines

Titles are in italic, first lines in roman